British Columbia's New North

How to Build Your Business, Respect Communities—and Prosper

Ramona Materi

Iza:
For always being
someone I look
forward to texting and
seeing when I come
home from the North.
With love and thanks,
imona

Melram Press

Editor: Lorn Kennedy
Cover Design: Madelyn Hambly
Interior Design: Stéphane Gibelin
Photo Credits: Unless otherwise noted, all photographs by Ramona Materi

Printed and bound in British Columbia, Canada by Printorium Bookworks

We hope you find this book a helpful source of information and welcome comments and suggestions. Email us at newnorth @ ingenia-consulting.com

Library and Archives Canada Cataloguing in Publication

Materi, Ramona, author
British Columbia's new north : how to build your business, respect communities--and prosper / Ramona Materi.

Includes bibliographical references.
Issued in print and electronic formats.
ISBN 978-0-9938593-6-6 (paperback).--ISBN 978-0-9938593-5-9 (epub).--
ISBN 978-0-9938593-4-2 (mobi)

1. British Columbia, Northern--Commerce. 2. British Columbia, Northern--Economic conditions. 3. New business enterprises--British Columbia, Northern. 4. Success in business--British Columbia, Northern. I. Title.

HC117.B8M42 2015   330.9711'8   C2015-902031-X
                                               C2015-902032-8

Published by Melram Press

1 3 5 7 9 10 8 6 4 2

Interested in knowing more?

Contact newnorth @ ingenia-consulting.com to find out more about the author, tour dates, how to book a workshop or presentation, or to order *British Columbia's New North* directly from the author.

Contents

Foreword

I came to Prince George and Northern British Columbia twenty years ago. I regarded it then, and even more so now, as a land of opportunity. British Columbia is rich in resources and enjoys enviable prosperity. Much of this wealth comes from the North and has been developed by generation after generation of entrepreneurs willing to take risks and work hard. This generation can follow in their footsteps and rise to the challenge of new opportunities. We are living at a time when major investments are being contemplated and made to transform existing industries, develop new industries, and expand fundamental infrastructures to enable northern British Columbians to benefit from today's global economy. It is a time for the emerging generation of entrepreneurs to embrace new ideas and create new enterprises both for their personal benefit and for British Columbia as a whole.

British Columbia's New North is a book for these times. Since 2011, Ramona Materi has been engaging regularly with business, governments, Aboriginal people, and non-profit organizations throughout the North. She has consulted in Northwest and Northeast British Columbia and created strategies for the solid wood, mining, and natural gas sectors. Ramona has worked with First Nations and Métis people and developed an educational strategy for an Aboriginal institution. She created workshops on attracting immigrants to the region. For this book, she has interviewed dozens of people in the North and elsewhere. Ramona knows firsthand the challenges and opportunities for business in the North, and she understands our need to attract new firms to open in our communities. *British Columbia's New North* is her contribution to that effort.

I welcome the creation of this practical, detailed guide for anyone thinking of establishing or expanding a business in the North. Crucially, it starts with an introduction to its people; those in the larger communities as well as its first inhabitants, the First Nations. The book includes invaluable information on the products and services that major projects require—and the commercial needs of the communities that will maintain these projects in the future. There's good guidance on travelling and living in the North and some solid advice from local companies on the keys to commercial and community success. It's current, it's accurate, and it's a good read.

I, too, have some experience with building an organization in the North. As the President of the University of Northern British Columbia from 1995 to 2006 and 2008 to 2009, I oversaw a period of tremendous growth at the University. My colleagues and I worked to establish the Northern Medical Program and the Northern Sport Centre. These initiatives have benefited people throughout the North and have increased its attractiveness to newcomers. Businesses thrive in strong communities and the University, its programs, and, most importantly, its graduates are an integral part of our economy today and tomorrow.

It's the North's time now and there's not a moment to waste. Major projects are starting up and business opportunities abound. *British Columbia's New North* is a powerful call to companies to seize a chance to prosper and contribute to our vibrant and growing northern communities. I hope it will be read by entrepreneurs and small business leaders all over our country, and globally, and that many will be inspired, as I was in 1995, to head north.

Dr. Charles J. Jago, MC, O.BC, LL.D. (hon), Ph.D.
Prince George, British Columbia

Terrace. British Columbia. Totem by Stan Bevan, Titus Auckland, and Ken Hans.

There is something bigger than fact: the underlying spirit, all it stands for, the mood, the vastness, the wildness.

Emily Carr, Artist and Writer, on British Columbia

Fraser Lake, British Columbia

Bountiful harvests

1 Agriculture plays an important role in the Northeast's economy; having almost one-third of British Columbia's farmland. It is primarily a grain and oilseed growing area, producing wheat, canola, barley, and hay crops, as well as cattle ranching. Honey is also an important crop. In the Northwest, ranching predominates.

Fly-in, fly-out camps

2 Companies bring workers to and from a construction or permanent work camp on a rotating schedule. Staff may work some weeks on and other weeks off. The employer provides transportation, accommodations, food, health care, and other services on-site. The camp services industry is growing in the North.

Grain silos, Dawson Creek, British Columbia

Farrell Creek Natural Gas Camp, Northeast British Columbia

Northern Lights College, Fort St. John, British Columbia

Kemess Mine landing strip near Smithers, British Columbia

Outside Terrace, British Columbia

Natural gas service rig used for training

3 In 2012, BC's natural gas sector employed over 13 thousand people, mostly in services to the sector. Many thousands more may be required to fill the need for gas for proposed liquefied natural gas plants and domestic customers.

Remote mining sites

4 The North has major deposits of coal, gold, silver, copper, zinc, rare earths, and other minerals. The town of Smithers is home to numerous exploration companies. New mines continue to open in British Columbia, including Red Chris in 2015.

Forestry: A mainstay of the rural economy

5 Forest companies buy billions of dollars in services, including accounting, environmental, engineering, consulting, information technology, and more. Opportunities exist for value-added wood product firms.

Alaska Highway, Northeast British Columbia

Tachik Lake, Vanderhoof, BC Photo: Kismenio Somcio

Huge demand for infrastructure

6 Governments are spending billions to upgrade roads, airports, schools, hospitals, and other public infrastructure in the North. Railways and private port owners are also investing heavily to increase capacity to move coal, forest products, grains, and other commodities.

New Canadians—New Homes

7 Increasing numbers of immigrants are moving North, for business opportunities and jobs. Since 2004, many immigrants to British Columbia have come from China, India, and the Philippines. Fort St. John (Filipino), Prince George (Punjabi), and Prince Rupert (Vietnamese) have significant immigrant communities.

Skeena River near Kitwanga, BC

A land and its peoples

First Nations people were the first inhabitants of the North; the Skeena and Nass Rivers were major fisheries and trade routes. The British Columbian and Canadian governments have engaged in treaty negotiations with First Nations since 1992; the Nisga'a Lisims Government signed the first treaty under that process in 1998.

Suspension bridge in Gitwinksihlkw, Nisga'a Territory

Near Dawson Creek, British Columbia

I am optimistic as we look forward to tomorrow....We are facing a generational opportunity, and we are going to lead Canada into the next century.

British Columbia Premier Christy Clark, speaking to the Vancouver Board of Trade

Introduction

A book is a device to ignite the imagination.

Alan Bennett

Have you ever thought of heading north? With the unprecedented number of anticipated major projects in Northern British Columbia, the opportunities for business are enormous. The provincial government's 2014 Major Projects Inventory outlines potentially billions of dollars of investment in the region. Projects include a hydro dam, major pipelines, liquefied natural gas plants, mines, wind farms, and more. These activities will generate a multitude of contracts for companies, large and small.

Achieving business success in the North can be challenging. Skilled workers are in short supply, logistics and supply lines are long, the climate can be harsh and the infrastructure limited. Recent court decisions related to First Nations and their territorial rights have increased the importance of working effectively with them. As well, while people unfamiliar with the region may speak simply of "the North," it is actually two or even three distinct regions: the Northeast, North Central, and the Northwest. The economic and social histories, climate, and terrain of these areas are different. Doing business in the region requires an understanding of their similarities and distinctiveness.

Tips:

Look for these boxes throughout the book for quick tips, as well as expert advice and northern perspectives.

The Book's Approach

British Columbia's New North provides up-to-date, essential information for businesses about positioning their firms to prosper in the North in the decade ahead. Drawing upon thorough secondary research and extensive interviews with company and government officials in the North and elsewhere, the book is a practical overview and business guide. Its goal is to help you understand the basics of operating in this new environment, so that your company, and the North, can prosper.

There's no single road map to success in the North. Instead, I've tried to give you the next best thing: sound advice, insider knowledge, and important background, drawn from interviews with people living in the region and those who do business there. As well, I've blended in tips and ideas from my years consulting in the North.

You'll also benefit from the advice and guidance from experts in various fields, including Aboriginal relations, health and safety, and immigration law. You'll hear from the locals, as they explain the reasons they choose to live in the North, and learn their perspectives on key economic issues.

By following the advice in the book, you'll have a better shot at plotting your course and discovering your own piece of business in BC's North—and the rewards it brings.

1. Who is the book for?

If you're an entrepreneur or an established owner of a small or medium enterprise (SME) looking to do business in Northern British Columbia, this book is for you. If you're a business investor, you'll discover these pages have a lot of information to help identify sectors where companies can be expected to do well. And if you're just curious and want to learn more about this vital and vibrant region, a read through these chapters will give you a great feel for and solid understanding of the North's economy and its people.

2. What's in the book?

British Columbia's New North is jam-packed with practical information and is structured as follows.

Part 1, Getting Oriented, offers:

- **The North Today**—A brief introduction to the region's economy, followed by business snapshots of nine communities that will serve as economic centres in the years ahead.

- **Aboriginal Peoples**—Two chapters, with the first providing a brief economic history of Aboriginal Peoples in the North. The second examines their business dealings today and has tips and practical advice from experienced executives and Aboriginal people on working effectively in today's changing business environment.

- **A Dynamic Decade**—An overview of major projects related to Liquefied Natural Gas, pipelines, and hydroelectricity. The chapter highlights the types of business goods and services these projects will require. In addition, it discusses contracting and health and safety requirements.

Nass River, Nisga'a Territory

Part 2, Staking Your Claim, has chapters on:

- **Travelling and Living in the North**—For people new to the region.

- **A Business Roadmap**—Positions your firm for doing business in the North. Includes information on effective websites and recruitment and retention of staff (including Temporary Foreign Workers and provincial and federal immigration programs). Experts in Aboriginal recruitment and immigration law provide valuable insights.

- **Hit the Ground Running**—21.5 business tips from the locals on steps you can take to increase your success.

The *Appendices* include:

- Contact details for community and Aboriginal economic development offices in Northern British Columbia

- Sample job description for a construction worker

- Sample job interview questions

- Notes

- Bibliography

3. How to use the book

You can go through the book from start to finish, or pick a chapter exploring an industry or theme of pressing interest. I've written each chapter so that it can stand alone and repeated key, relevant information in different places. Whatever the approach, by reading *British Columbia's New North,* you'll gain knowledge and ideas that will put you a step ahead of your competitors—and have no doubt, today, many businesses and investors are actively searching for and finding great opportunities in British Columbia's New North.

Let's get started!

PART 1

Getting Oriented

Terrace, British Columbia

CHAPTER 1

The North Today
Economic Basics & Major Communities

Behind every small business, there's a story worth knowing.
All the corner shops in our towns and cities, the restaurants,
cleaners, hardware stores - these didn't come out of nowhere.

Paul Ryan

This chapter provides some facts on the province of British Columbia and defines Northern British Columbia. It also introduces the main components of the traditional economy. Finally, it introduces you to some of the major towns and communities in the North, through brief economic snapshots.

British Columbia is the westernmost of Canada's provinces. It is bordered by the Pacific Ocean to the west, the province of Alberta to the east, Northwest Territories, Yukon Territory, and the state of Alaska to the north, and Washington State to the south. The province is famed for its natural beauty, as reflected in its Latin motto, "Splendor sine occasu" (translation "Splendour without Diminishment") or today's tourist slogan, "Super Natural British Columbia."

Table 1.1: British Columbia Fast Facts

Population	Provincial population is over 4.5 million, which is mostly concentrated in the Greater Vancouver region (population 2.4 million) and Greater Victoria, (population 355,000). In 2013, the population of Canada was 35 million (2013).[1]
Capital city	Victoria, on Vancouver Island
Total area	944,735 km sq / 364,764 mi sq (For comparison, the total area of France is 640,679 km sq)
Political History	Entered Canadian confederation in 1871, on the promise that a railway would be built to link the province to the rest of Canada. The first premier was Victoria lawyer John Foster McCreight.
Government	Levels of government include provincial, regional districts, and municipal. The local government system is unique in Canada because, in addition to the municipal governments, the province is comprised of 27 regional districts. Their boundaries are large and span nearly all of BC. Each regional district is divided into smaller areas called electoral areas. So, depending on your business and location, you may need to work with four levels of government!

Defining Northern British Columbia

British Columbia is big. Defining Northern BC is a challenge; people in one town may regard another community as being in the central or southern part of the province. Residents of those places will exclaim that they are as much a part of the North as the others. It's complicated.

For the purposes of this book, Northern British Columbia includes everything from Prince George, north to the Yukon, and from the Alberta border to Haida Gwaii (see Page 12). As can be seen, hundreds of kilometers separate communities; the North is an enormous place. The book further subdivides the region into Northwest British Columbia, which includes the towns and important business centres of Prince Rupert, Kitimat, and Terrace, North Central (Prince George and Smithers), and the Northeast (Fort Nelson, Fort St. John, and Dawson Creek). The population of this entire area, in 2013, was approximately 264,000 people.[2]

Northern British Columbia is so huge that, if dropped on a map of Europe, it would more than cover France. As a region, it's geographically larger than the state of California. The entire United Kingdom would take up only half of it, or you could place all of Japan into it with room left over. Yet only four main roads and a couple of railways frame this vast Northern wilderness. (See Chapter 5, Travelling and Living in the North, for more details.)

The Northern Economy Today – Business Building Blocks

The North, historically, has been a resource-based economy. It is a vast treasure trove of timber, minerals, coal, and natural gas – and large rivers for damming. The excellent *Investing in Place*, by professors at the University of Northern British Columbia, provides a thorough overview of the history of the northern economy, particularly since the 1940s. Below is some brief information to introduce you to the major industries and activities that form the foundation blocks of the current northern economy.

Forestry

From the 1950s to the 1980s, BC's economy rose and sank on the fortunes of forestry. The provincial economy is now more diversified, but forestry remains the economic backbone of many small communities in Northern British Columbia. Forest products remain the largest source of export earnings for the province. In the North, the timber supply near Fort Nelson remains ample, with large spruce forests. In the interior near Prince George, largely as a result of diminishing timber supplies caused by a pine beetle infestation, the industry will be shrinking, as it has in the Northwest. The forest products cluster purchases goods and services from a vast array of businesses. Companies procure billions of dollars in services, including accounting, environmental, engineering, consulting, information technology, and customs services. Forest products companies also purchase maintenance services and machinery and equipment.

Agriculture

Although visitors tend to think of British Columbia in terms of mountains, lakes and forests, the North, like other parts of the province, has a thriving agricultural sector. The Northeast, for example, has about 1,600 farms and ranches and has excellent soils, allowing it to grow fruits, vegetables, and cereal and forage crops that otherwise grow only in southern areas. The agriculture sector is key to the region and to British Columbia as a whole. According to the North Peace Economic Commission, the Northeast grows almost 90 per cent of the province's grain and 95 per cent of its canola. As well, the Peace is one of the best areas in the world for producing quality grass seeds. Honey production is also bountiful, with the region usually providing 30 per cent of the province's honey crops.

Livestock production in the North is also strong. Ranchers raise traditional beef and dairy cattle, sheep, hogs, goats, and horses. In the Northeast, they are also increasingly diversifying into game farming of bison, reindeer, and exotic livestock, including llama, alpaca, fox, ostrich, emu, and wild boar. In fact, ranchers in the Northeast have some of the province's largest bison herds, producing nearly three quarters of British Columbia's bison.

The organic market is important, too. An increasing number of Northeast farms are producing certified organic beef, bison, poultry, hogs, eggs, wheat, barley, herbs, hay, oil seeds, peas, as well as table and seed potatoes.

Many farmers in British Columbia are now nearing retirement and in many cases there are insufficient new entrants into the industry to replace them. In 2011, 54% of BC farm operators were over 55 years old – up from 45% in 2006 – while only 5.4% were under 35 to 40.

Natural gas

British Columbia's natural gas industry dates from the mid-20th century. In 1948, drillers made a major gas discovery near Fort St. John in the Northeast; by 1957, a new gas plant at Taylor (near Fort St. John) processed gas to transmit to the Pacific Northwest by pipeline for sale to Canadian and American customers.

Currently, the majority of natural gas industry activity, including exploration and production and natural gas processing, takes place in the Northeast region of BC. Activity is focused on four basins including three north of Fort Nelson (Liard, Horn River, and Cordova Embayment), and one situated near Fort St. John and Dawson Creek (Montney).

In 2003, the provincial government introduced a royalty program called the Summer Drilling Credit Program that encouraged year-round drilling – and the boom was on for the region. In addition, changes in technology introduced in 2005 have allowed companies to access gas trapped in shale, increasing British Columbia's marketable shale gas reserve to an estimated 2,900 trillion cubic feet. Industry investment almost quadrupled between 2000 and 2010, increasing from $1.8 billion to $7.1 billion.

Based on the amount of gas industry is able to recover and increased activity, British Columbia has over 150 years worth of natural gas supply.[3] BC currently produces 1.4 trillion cubic feet of natural gas annually. In 2012, British Columbia's natural gas industry employed about 13,000 workers across three subsectors: oil and gas services, exploration and production (E&P), and natural gas pipelines.

The current challenge for industry is that prices for natural gas in the United States have been dropping steadily since 2009. Using the same new methods of releasing gas from shale, the US has decreased its import requirements. As a result, BC producers must find new markets.

Since 2010, companies have been exploring the feasibility of building liquefied natural gas (LNG) plants on the coast of Northwest BC. The idea would be to drill for gas in the Northeast, then, via new pipelines, transport it to the North Coast. There, companies would build LNG export plants, which liquefy natural gas by cooling it. The plants then pump the LNG into specialized tankers and ship it to offshore markets such as Japan and China.

The construction of these plants will enable the province to diversify its export market and take advantage of the rapidly expanding Asian market. Direct employment in BC's natural gas industry is projected to grow from 12,000 workers in 2012 to over 40,000 workers by 2035, largely as a result of the LNG related activity.

Rio Tinto Alcan Aluminum Smelter

The Rio Tinto Alcan (RTA) aluminum smelter in Kitimat, in the Northwest of British Columbia, has been a mainstay of the coastal economy since its completion in 1954. The town of Kitimat was purpose-built to house the plant's workers. The plant has its own source of power, the result of its private dam on the Nechako River. According to RTA estimates, the smelter contributes about a quarter of a billion dollars annually to the Canadian economy, of which about half stays in British Columbia.

Announced in 2011, the smelter underwent a $5 billion modernization program, intended to equip it with state of the art equipment to double production and reduce emissions by 50 per cent. The global construction firm Bechtel oversaw a workforce that reached over 3,000 people. Start-up of the new smelter was expected in late 2015; the modernized plant will employ about 1,000 workers.

Mining

Gross mining revenues for the mining industry in British Columbia were $8.2 billion in 2014. More than half of Canada's exploration and mining companies are based in British Columbia, which has the largest concentration of exploration companies and geoscience professionals in the world. Thanks to its diverse geology, the province is rich in high quality mineral resources, with the North an important region for the industry. The province produces and exports a significant amount of copper, gold, silver, lead, zinc, molybdenum, coal, and industrial minerals every year. As well, the mining industry is one of the largest private sector employers of First Nations people in British Columbia.

Coal remains, on a value of product basis, the most important provincial mining resource as shown in the chart below, with data taken from 2011. Total product value from BC mining in 2011 came to about $8.6 billion. Coal production comes from two main areas - the East Kootenays, and Northeast BC, with the largest resource located in the Northeast (800 million tonnes versus 560 million tonnes).

Much of the coal produced is shipped to the West Coast terminals such as Prince Rupert via rail and from there to Asian markets.

The Northwest has large deposits of copper and smaller reserves of gold and molybdenum, zinc, and other minerals. Most of it is mined through large-scale open pit mines and some underground mines. With the opening of the Northwest Transmission Line in 2014, mines now had the electricity they needed to operate and more are expected to be developed. While the BC industry as a whole faced a downturn in 2014, with coal mines closing in the

the Northeast, the revenues from gold, copper, zinc and molybdenum rose.[4]

The provincial government strongly supports the mining industry and has laid out strategies to increase the number of new mines and expand existing ones. Mines play an important part in the North's economy, with properties such as Mount Milligan, Red Chris, Au Rico Gold, Kitsault, and others providing well paying jobs and numerous ongoing service contracts to local suppliers. New mines continue to be constructed and present opportunities for contractors as they are built. Each year in May, the industry hosts Minerals North, a conference that moves around the region and presents the latest information on activities and opportunities in the northern mining sector.

Figure 1: Product Value from British Columbia Mining 2011[5]

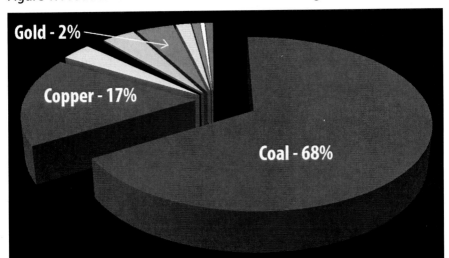

Table 1.2: Provincial/Regional Information Sources for Business

Invest Northwest, North Central, Northeast BC investnorthwestbc.ca investnorthcentralbc.ca investnortheastbc.ca	Websites for each of the regions in the North, outlining major economic opportunities. Each website provides specific and practical information in detail. Very useful.
Northern Development Initiative Trust www.northerndevelop ment.bc.ca	Northern Development Initiative Trust focusses on being a catalyst for Northern BC to build a strong and diversified economy. It offers incentives for investors and business looking to locate and expand manufacturing and value-added operations within Northern British Columbia. It has a helpful monthly newsletter.
Western Economic Diversification Canada www.wd-deo.gc.ca	Canadian federal department responsible for economic development and diversification in Western Canada. It has a wide variety of useful programs for entrepreneurs.
Ministry of Jobs, Tourism, and Skills Training engage.gov.bc.ca/bcjobsplan	The Ministry is responsible for putting the BC Jobs Plan into action, to increase the province's economic competitiveness.
Trade and Invest British Columbia www.britishcolumbia.ca	Official trade and investment website for BC, helping international companies invest in British Columbia.

Port of Prince Rupert

The Port of Prince Rupert is a crucial hub in the transport of the resources that the North generates. As the Port Authority notes:

> Lumber and pulp from communities such as Smithers are being shipped through Fairview Container Terminal to growing markets in China. Wood pellets from Houston and Burns Lake are moving through the Westview Wood Pellet Terminal. Wheat, canola, and other grains from Dawson Creek and Fort St. John are travelling through Prince Rupert Grain's terminal on their way to feed families in Mexico and Sri Lanka. Metallurgical coal from Tumbler Ridge and Chetwynd is being shipped through Ridley Coal Terminal to steel factories in Korea and Japan.[6]

In 2014, the Port Authority released a five year economic impact study. It found that transportation of port-related exports and imports generates $1.2 billion in economic activity annually. From 2009 to 2014, port employment doubled to 3,320 full-time jobs. When indirect and induced employment is taken into account, the port is responsible for nearly 6,200 jobs, of which 43 per cent are located outside of Prince Rupert.

A major advantage of Prince Rupert is that it offers the fastest access for vessels travelling between Asia and North America and an efficient rail link to the hinterland. As the North grows, more shipping companies are seeing value in its location. In April 2015, for example, DP World Ltd., the Dubai government-owned ports operator, bought the Fairview Container Terminal for $580-million. The terminal is expanding its capacity from 850,000 TEU to 1.35 million TEU.

The Major Communities

The North, while sparsely populated, has vibrant communities spread throughout. To help you get a better feel for them and the business opportunities they offer, the following pages provide brief economic snapshots of eight of these cities and towns. If you're thinking of doing business in the North, they are great places to start!

These centres will play a major role in the North's economic development. Some are longtime commercial hubs (Fort St. John, for example, is the oldest European settlement in BC), others are becoming more important because of major projects that will be located near them.

Some of these communities have prepared "Investment Ready Community Profiles," usually available on their official websites. These documents provide detailed statistics on workforces, land availability, and other useful information for potential investors and employers.

Figure 2: Map of British Columbia Showing Major Communities

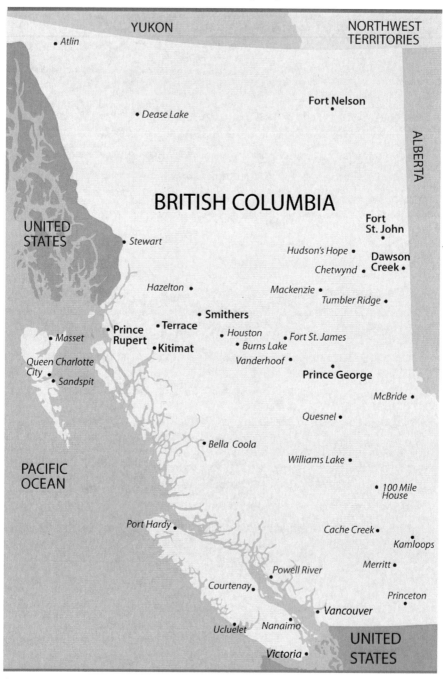

(Communities in bold are profiled on the following pages.)

Business Opportunities in the Towns—A Sample

A great way to understand some of the business opportunities available in northern communities is to review excerpts from articles that appeared in newspapers from 2012 to 2015.

Fort St. John will need 'more of everything': Millennials hear the call of B.C.'s north

The recent Fort St. John Energy Expo gave an indication of an emerging northern B.C. boom town in the midst of the liquefied natural gas (LNG) industry.

"Fort St. John is the centre of it all," said keynote speaker Bill Gwozd, "This is where the gas is going to start from. Production is going to grow. Transportation is going to grow. You're going to need more people. You're going to need more of everything."

Business in Vancouver, July 15, 2014

Lessons from B.C.'s 'Northern Capital': Be flexible, diversify, seize opportunities

In Prince George, we found a city in transition. Known for its high-paying blue-collar jobs, "PG" is now attracting entrepreneurs from the information industries: engineering firms and environmental consultants to serve the big resource companies and help them become more competitive, as well as IT startups.

Financial Post, September 23, 2012

Terrace lands Chinese manufacturer

The City of Terrace has sold 1,056 acres at its Skeena Industrial Park to a Chinese investment company that plans to open an alfalfa protein extraction factory, bringing 170 new jobs. "Taisheng expects construction of the first factory could begin in 2017 or 2018," a city release states. The City of Terrace and the Kitselas First Nation are joint venture partners in the Park.

Western Investor, July 16, 2014

Chains find big opportunities in small towns

Prestige and brand visibility can entice entrepreneurs to open a store at a high-traffic intersection of a large urban centre. Expanding rapidly by targeting underserved small towns, however, can be a more profitable strategy.

The key to success in smaller centres is to have a brand that has mass appeal. Companies that have found success in small towns are careful to appeal to a broad base, even if they locate in boom towns filled with wealthier transient workers.

"Often we're the nicest restaurant in town," said CEO Mike Cordoba, who has expanded his chain to 22 restaurants. He has sold an additional 25 locations that he expects will open in within five to eight years. "In these smaller towns, there's hardly any [chain restaurants], so when you put in a Mr Mikes, people get really excited and go, 'Wow, we've got a steakhouse but it's actually a casual steakhouse.'"

Business in Vancouver May 4, 2014

The industries that stand to gain, and lose, if (a major pipeline) gets built

There's also BC Hydro's proposed Site C Dam, which has an estimated price tag of $8 billion, and the buildout of the region's Liquefied Natural Gas assets, which will involve billions more in spending. Add it all up, according to PI Financial's Jason Zandberg, and it could spell the mother of all labour crunches. It's great for businesses on the other end of that equation. That's because increasing wages will almost certainly translate into increased sales at restaurants, on truck accessories and a range of other indulgences—and that's in addition to the $800 million that will already be spent on transportation, equipment, food and hospitality in local communities. "Labour will win out with higher wages, and so will the communities where they spend their money—all the goods and services that are purchased around the area," Zandberg says. "We'll see real estate prices going up in these northern communities, and there will definitely be winners as more income flows into the labour pool."

BC Business, November 2014

Terrace's business cycle ready to enter busy time

Below is a representative sampling of recent activity in Terrace.

Simson Maxwell
The firm, which sells as well as services industrial engines, is about to open a local branch.

"We see a lot of potential in the area with LNG and other development," says company official Ben Beeching of its decision to locate in Terrace.

Bandstra
Work at Bandstra has already started on a 10,000 square foot warehouse that will more than double the size of the company's current warehouse space.

"We were getting pretty tight for space," said Sid Bandstra of the decision to expand.

The company is anticipating hiring several people as summer nears, mostly for its moving business but also for freight transportation with the latter prospect depending on general economic activity.

Andrew Sheret

Andrew Sheret, which sells plumbing, heating, HVAC and other supplies, is making Terrace its 22nd sales location within the province.

"We can see the growth in the area and believe there's an opportunity there," explains company vice president Eric Findlay of its expansion decision.

Dulux Paints

Another new company to the area is Dulux Paints.

"It's because that's where the economic activity is," says Dave Rimmer, who's responsible for the company's western Canadian corporate stores. "We looked at the economic indicators and we knew we needed to be in northern B.C. That's where we think we should be in anticipation of the next five years, 10 years."

MacCarthy Motors

Terrace's General Motors dealership has also expanded by putting in a new storage area for tires and parts in response, a total of an extra 5,000 square feet.

"Our business has picked up a lot in the last 24 months," said assistant controller Kevin MacCarthy. "Tires are a big part of our business now. We ran out of room for storing them."

Terrace Standard April 9, 2015

Long-Term Growth…for Tourism in Northern B.C.

Higher visitor numbers and a sharp spike in inquiries at Prince George's information centres have Tourism Prince George CEO Aidan Kelly enthusiastic about long-term growth in the tourism and hospitality sector.

The upswing in the natural resources sector has reinforced Prince George's profile as a hub for business tourism, but higher interest in outdoor recreation from long-haul "rubber tire travellers" (tourists that come on two- to three-week trips) is also helping the important leisure travel market, according to Kelly. He says that higher traffic from leisure and business travellers has led to a compound 18 per cent growth in hotel revenues.

BC Business June 17, 2013

Original Joe's takes a pad (in Dawson Creek)

Bosa Development confirmed this week that Original Joe's Restaurant & Bar is planning a move into one of the two unfinished buildings. The Calgary-based restaurant chain, fresh off opening new outlets in Fort St. John and Grande Prairie in recent months, will move into an 8,400-square-foot space.

Alaska Highway News February 20, 2015

Central British Columbia – **Prince George**

Location: 787 km north of Vancouver, 70 minute flight

Population: 85,996 (2014 BC Stats, Census Agglomeration Area)

Key Industries: Wholesale/retail, health care, manufacturing, construction

Overview

Prince George serves as the supply and service centre for industry activities across the central and northern regions of British Columbia, creating opportunities for local businesses in many service sectors.

Business Organizations

- Initiatives Prince George www.initiativespg.com
- Prince George Chamber of Commerce pgchamber.bc.ca
- Community Futures Fraser-Fort George cfdc.bc.ca
- Innovation Central Society innovationcentral.ca
- Startup Prince George www.startupprincegeorge.ca
- Prince George Construction Association www.pgca.bc.ca
- Canadian Home Builders' Association of Northern BC chbanorthernbc.ca

Aboriginal Peoples in the Region

- Lheidli T'enneh www.lheidli.ca
- Carrier Sekani Tribal Council www.carriersekani.ca
- Prince George Métis Community Association www.pgmca.ca

Proposed Major Projects in the Region

- Hart North Industrial Site, Prince George Economic Development Corp./Regional District of Fraser-Fort George
- Prince George Global Logistics Park ($382 million)

- Mount George Wind Park, Northland Power Inc. ($100 million)
- Giscome Quarry and Lime Project, Graymont Western Canada ($130 million)

Business Opportunities

Initiatives Prince George (www.initiativespg.com) has created short profiles for investment opportunities in nine sectors, including:

- construction
- energy and bioenergy
- forestry
- healthcare and education
- manufacturing
- mining
- professional and technical services
- tourism
- transportation and warehousing

Transportation

- International airport, rail, passenger rail, Highways 16 and 97

Near Prince George, British Columbia

Commercial Real Estate

- Prince George offers industrial and commercial real estate opportunities, low development cost charges, and competitive tax rates.
- The City's Downtown Incentives Program encourages new residential and commercial development.

Local Resources

- CKPG TV ckpg.com
- Prince George Citizen www.princegeorgecitizen.com
- Opinion 250 www.250news.com
- CBC Radio – Daybreak North www.cbc.ca/daybreaknorth
- University of Northern BC www.unbc.ca
- College of New Caledonia www.cnc.bc.ca
- Sprott Shaw Community College sprottshaw.com
- Immigrant and Multicultural Services Society of Prince George www.imss.ca

Why I love Prince George

Baljit Sethi, Executive Director, Immigrant and Multicultural Services Society

Prince George has the facilities of a big city and the peaceful and friendly environment of a medium-sized town. It is good city to raise a young family. One has more time for the family rather than spending time in your car trying to reach home. To own a house is easier than paying rent. Prince George is a very friendly community. I love this city.

Unique Prince George

Prince George serves as a northern health care hub, with a university teaching hospital and regional cancer care facility. In February 2015, the Canada Winter Games took place in Prince George, leaving the City with world-class ice rinks, ski trails, and modernized recreation centres.

Northwest British Columbia – **Smithers**

Location: 1,153 km northwest of Vancouver, 105 minute flight

Population: 5,400 (2011 Statistics Canada Census)

Key Industries: Forestry, construction, tourism, agriculture, mineral exploration

Overview

Located in the resource-rich Bulkley Valley, Smithers' strong forestry, agriculture, and tourism industries are the base of its economic prosperity. It is also a centre for the mining exploration industry, hosting a cluster of support industries.

Business Organizations

- Smithers Chamber of Commerce smitherschamber.com
- Bulkley Valley Economic Development Association www.bveda.ca
- Community Futures Nadina www.cfnadina.ca

Aboriginal Peoples in the Region

- Wet'suwet'en Nation www.wetsuweten.com
- Moricetown Band www.moricetown.ca

Transportation

- Airport, rail, passenger rail
- Yellowhead Highway 16

Business Opportunities

- Health care – Eastern and Western practitioners. Smithers serves the surrounding communities as well.
- Consultants to the natural resource industry
- The town has a small software development cluster

Proposed Major Projects

- Kemess Underground Copper-Gold Mine, AuRico Gold ($437 million)

Commercial Real Estate

- 132 acres rezoned industrial at Smithers Regional Airport
- Some vacant space in a redeveloped mall
- Bare land with flexible zoning for commercial and light industrial—within town
- Manufacturing facilities are available

Local Resources

- CFTKTV Terrace www.cftktv.com
- Moose FM CFBV.Moosefm.com
- Smithers Interior News www.interior-news.com
- Smithers Community Services Association www.scsa.ca
- North West Community College—Smithers Campus www.nwcc.bc.ca
- Town of Smithers www.smithers.ca

Unique Smithers

Smithers has adopted an alpine theme, requiring downtown buildings to be constructed in an alpine façade style. Many skilled trades people live in Smithers. Some commute to work camps outside the town.

Smithers has twice the number of medical doctors needed for its size and the second most PhDs per capita in BC, after Victoria. It's an entrepreneurial place, with a median income of $64,000 in 2015.

Northeast British Columbia – **Dawson Creek**

Location: 1,190 km northeast of Vancouver, 120 minute flight

Population: 12,496 (2014 BC Stats, Census Agglomeration Area)

Key Industries: Agriculture, oil and gas, forestry, mining, tourism

Overview

Dawson Creek is in a region where oil and gas, large scale maintenance, and construction projects will provide a strong foundation for economic growth. As a hub for highways connecting the Northeast with Alberta and Alaska, it serves as a service and residential centre for the South Peace region.

Business Organizations

- South Peace Economic Development Commission www.southpeacebc.ca
- Community Futures www.communityfutures.biz
- Dawson Creek Chamber of Commerce www.dawsoncreekchamber.ca

Aboriginal Peoples in the Region

- Northeast Métis
- West Moberly www.westmo.org
- Saulteau First Nations www.saulteau.com
- Blueberry River First Nations
- Doig River First Nations treaty8.bc.ca/communities/doig-river-first-nation
- Treaty 8 First Nations treaty8.bc.ca
- Kelly Lake Métis Community

Transportation

- Airport, rail, Highway 97, Highways 2 and 49 to Alberta

Major Projects

Under Construction in 2015

- Dawson Creek/Chetwynd Area Transmission (DCAT), BC Hydro ($296 million)

Proposed

- LNG Plant, Alta Gas Ltd. ($250 million)

- Merrick Mainline Pipeline, TransCanada Corp. ($160 million)

- Coastal GasLink Pipeline Project ($4 billion)

- Meikle Windy Energy Project, Pattern Energy ($400 million)

- Blue Fuel Project, Aeolis Wind Power Corp. and Blue Fuel Energy Corp. ($3 billion)

Business Opportunities

- Retail

- Industrial services for major projects

Commercial Real Estate

- Commercial property values have been rising in Dawson Creek. Two new industrial parks are under development in 2015, adding to the three existing parks.

- With many large projects still to arrive, the vacancy rate is already low with industrial property in high demand.

Local Resources

- Alaska Highway News www.alaskahighwaynews.ca

- North East News www.northeastnews.ca

- Dawson Creek Literacy Society www.dcliteracynow.ca

- Northern Lights College www.nlc.bc.ca

Unique Dawson Creek

The 2,451 kilometre long Alaska Highway was built in 1942 with Dawson Creek as Mile 0. The discovery of oil and gas in the region in 1950 led to the incorporation of Dawson Creek as a city in 1958. Since 2003, the current shale gas boom has brought hundreds of new companies to the region.

Northeast British Columbia – **Fort Nelson**

Location: 1,602 km north of Vancouver, 225 minute (1 stop) flight

Population: 5,440 (2014 BC Stats, Northern Rockies Regional Municipality)

Key Industries: Natural gas, tourism, agriculture, forestry

Overview

Fort Nelson is the shale gas capital of Canada. The town is surrounded by an abundance of other natural resources including mixed boreal forests and an emerging agricultural sector. The Alaska Highway is an excellent transportation corridor and opens the area to tourism. Many major projects are forecasted in natural gas and construction.

Business Organizations

- Fort Nelson Chamber of Commerce
  www.fortnelsonchamber.com
- Northern Rockies Regional Municipality
  www.northernrockies.ca

Aboriginal Peoples in the Region

- Fort Nelson First Nation www.fortnelsonfirstnation.org
- Dene Tsaa Tse K'Nai First Nation (Prophet River First Nation)
- Kaska Dene
- Lower Post First Nation

Commercial Real Estate

- Industrial and commercial lots are available in various areas including Northern Rockies Light Industrial Park and BCR Industrial Park.
- Fort Nelson's natural gas industry attracts large oil and gas companies including EnCana, Nexen, and Imperial Oil.

Transportation

- Airport, rail
- Alaska Highway 97

Proposed Major Projects

- Horn River Basin Light Industrial Park, (phased development; partially complete) Northern Rockies Regional Municipality ($40 million)

Business Opportunities in Fort Nelson and Region

Fort Nelson mills produced significant volumes of Oriented Strand Board (OSB), plywood, and dimensional lumber, but operations stopped in 2008. This has left a large, diverse, untapped wood supply, offering substantial investment opportunities. See more at www.northernrockies.ca.

Local Resources

- Fort Nelson News www.fnnews.ca
- Alaska Highway News www.alaskahighwaynews.ca
- Fort Nelson Community Literacy Society fncls.com
- Northern Lights College, Fort Nelson Campus www.nlc.bc.ca
- Fort Nelson, Northern Rockies Regional Municipality www.northernrockies.ca

Unique Fort Nelson

The Northern Rocky Mountains area is the largest landscape without roads south of the 60th parallel. It has one of the richest and most varied wildlife ecosystems remaining in North America and has been called the Serengeti of the North.

Northeast British Columbia – **Fort St. John**

Location: 1,223 km northeast of Vancouver, 100 minute flight

Population: 29,739 (BC Stats 2014, Census Agglomeration Area)

Key Industries: Agriculture, natural gas, mining, tourism, forestry

Overview

Fort St. John's economy is built on the oil and gas, coal, hydroelectric, forestry, and agriculture sectors. The city is the largest regional service centre in Northeastern British Columbia, servicing over 60,000 people.

Business Organizations

- North Peace Economic Development Commission npedc.ca
- Invest in Northeast BC investnortheastbc.ca
- Community Futures www.communityfutures.ca
- Fort St. John Chamber of Commerce www.fsjchamber.com
- Economic Development www.fortstjohn.ca

Aboriginal Peoples in the Region

- Treaty 8 Association treaty8.bc.ca
- Blueberry River First Nations
- Doig River First Nations
  treaty8.bc.ca/communities/doig-river-first-nation
- Halfway River First Nation
  treaty8.bc.ca/communities/halfway-river-first-nation
- Métis Nation of BC www.mnbc.ca

Transportation

- Airport, rail
- Alaska Highway 97

Major Projects in the Region

Proposed

- Site C Clean Energy Project, BC Hydro ($9 billion)
- Hackney Hills Wind Park, Aeolis Wind Power Corporation ($850 million)
- Townsend Gas Processing Facility, AltaGas/Painted Pony Petroleum Ltd. ($350 million)
- Farrell Creek 88-I South Gas Plant, Talisman Energy Inc. ($250 million)
- Carbon Creek Mine, Cardero Resource Corp.
- Gething Coal Project, Canadian Kailuan Dehua Mines Ltd./Shandong Energy Feicheng Mining Group Co. Ltd. ($1.36 billion)
- Station 44 Town Centre, G8 Properties ($500 million)
- Taylor Wind Project, Taylor Wind Project Ltd. ($900 million)

Business Opportunities

- Retail—boutique, franchises, family focused (e.g. dog kennel)
- Restaurants
- Medical services
- Housing
- Landscaping firms
- Contractors to major project construction, asphalt plant

Commercial Real Estate

- Fort St. John is surrounded by an Agriculture Land Reserve and has a shortage of serviced commercial and industrial sites. Commercial property prices have doubled since 2012 to $25-29 per square foot in early 2015.
- Proposed Site C Dam and liquefied natural gas projects could increase demand.

Local Resources

- CJDC TV www.cjdctv.com
- Alaska Highway News www.alaskahighwaynews.ca
- The Northerner thenortherner.ca
- Energetic City energeticcity.ca
- S.U.C.C.E.S.S. Settlement and Business Centre (Immigrant services) www.successbc.ca
- Northern Lights College www.nlc.bc.ca
- University of Northern BC Peace River-Liard Campus www.unbc.ca/peace-river-liard

Unique Fort St. John

In 2011, the median age in Fort St. John was 30.6 years, compared to the median age of 41.9 years for BC. Its nick-name is "The Energetic City." Fort St. John has a large and growing Filipino community.

What impact has the drop in oil prices in 2014/2015 had on Fort St. John?

Moira Green is the Economic Development Officer for the City of Fort St. John.

The drop in oil and gas prices hasn't had a huge impact on us. Fort St. John tends to be quite protected from the commodity bumps in the market. There is some contraction and reorganization in the service world. Some contracts are being reviewed and rewritten. Companies that are heavily exposed, or have their parent firms heavily exposed in oil, are making changes to their operations.

But what happens is, the companies that are well organized, the A and B list firms, have a little nest egg of retained earnings which they're using to make acquisitions. They're using that money to make the hire they always wanted to make. So for those companies, this is a time of opportunity. There will be contraction and consolidation, which is ok and what happened in 2008. That year was tough and oil prices were low then too. If you ask people in the community here if there is short term pain, they'll say yes. Are they worried? Not at all. We have been to this rodeo before.

Northwest British Columbia – **Kitimat**

Location: 1,411 km northwest of Vancouver, 110 minute flight

Population: 8,452 (2014 BC Stats, District Municipality)

Key Industries: Manufacturing, retail, health care

Overview

Kitimat is a purpose-built town, home to the Rio Tinto Alcan aluminum smelter, which finished a large modernization program in 2015. The community is booming. Companies from around the world are planning investments in liquefied natural gas, shipping, and transportation industries in the coming decade.

Business Organizations

- Kitimat Economic Development Association keda.ca
- Kitimat Chamber of Commerce www.kitimatchamber.ca

Aboriginal Peoples in the Region

- Haisla First Nation haisla.ca

Major Projects

At permitting stage in 2015

- Terminal A Extension Project, Rio Tinto Alcan ($250 million)
- Kitimat Transmission Line, BC Hydro

Proposed

- Terminal A Extension Project, Rio Tinto Alcan ($250 million)
- Kitimat Clean Oil Refinery and Pipeline, Kitimat Clean Ltd. ($27 billion)
- Kitimat LNG, Chevron Canada/Woodside Petroleum Ltd.
- LNG Canada Facility, Shell, PetroChina, Korea Gas, Mitsubishi ($25 billion)

- Kitimat will be the end point of four major pipelines to supply the proposed LNG plants
- Douglas Channel LNG, Douglas Channel LNG Consortium ($450 million)
- Pacific Trail Pipeline, Chevron Canada ($5.8 billion)
- Coastal GasLink, TransCanada Corp. ($4 billion)
- Pacific Northern Gas Looping Project, Pacific Northern Gas ($130 million)

Transportation

- Port, rail, airport
- Highway 37 connects to Yellowhead Highway 16

Business Opportunities

- Supply and services to major project construction
- Local business owners are retiring. Restaurants, convenience stores, and hotels are for sale.
- Support services for hotels

Commercial Real Estate

- A wide range of commercial, retail, and service land uses are allowed in the City Centre.
- Many greenfield and brownfield industrial sites in Kitimat are pre-zoned for industrial activity. Areas exist for automotive, industrial services, retail use, heavy manufacturing, and port related activity.
- The developing liquefied natural gas sector has pushed up prices on commercial properties in Kitimat. The Commercial Zone Revitalization Tax Exemption Program encourages new construction and renovations by offering a five-year tax exemption on the increase in assessed value, to a maximum of $2 million.

Local Resources

- Northern Sentinel www.northernsentinel.com
- Tourism Kitimat www.tourismkitimat.ca
- Kitimat Community Services www.kitimatcommunityservices.ca
- Kitimat Valley Institute www.kvic.ca
- Kitimat Website www.kitimat.ca

Unique Kitimat

Kitimat is Western Canada's third largest port and the busiest private port. It is deep sea and ice-free year round. One in five residents of Kitimat has a first language other than English, according to the 2011 Census.

Photo: Tourism Kitimat

Northwest British Columbia – **Prince Rupert**

Location: 1,500 km northwest of Vancouver, 120 minute flight

Population: 12,496 (BC Stats 2014, Census Agglomeration Area)

Key Industries: Services, manufacturing, transportation, and warehousing

Overview

Prince Rupert is a major port city with important economic connections with Asia. Billions of dollars are committed for regional investment in sustainable energy, liquefied natural gas, and port expansion. There are major business opportunities available.

Business Organizations

- Prince Rupert and Port Edward Economic Development Corporation (PREDC) www.predc.com
- Prince Rupert & District Chamber of Commerce princerupertchamber.ca
- Community Futures of the Pacific Northwest communityfuturesprincerupert.com

Aboriginal Peoples in the Region

- Tsimshian First Nations, including Metlakatla www.metlakatla.ca
- Laxkwalaams laxkwalaams.ca
- Prince Rupert is bordered by the traditional lands of the Gitxsan, Nisga'a, Haida, and Heiltsuk.

Transportation

- Port, airport, rail, passenger train, BC Ferries
- Yellowhead Highway 16

Proposed Major Projects

- Pacific Northwest LNG, Petronas/Progress/JAPEX ($11 billion)
- Bitumen Refinery, Pacific Future Energy Corp. ($10 billion)
- Woodside Energy LNG, Woodside Energy Holdings Pty Ltd. ($10 billion)
- Fairview Container Terminal Expansion, DP World/Prince Rupert Port Authority/CN Rail ($650 million)
- Prince Rupert Gas Transmission Project, TransCanada Corp. ($5 billion)
- Watson Island Industrial Site Redevelopment
- Prince Rupert Potash Terminal, Canpotex Terminals Ltd. ($775 million)
- Tsimshian Peninsula Access Project/Tuck Inlet Road, Prince Rupert City ($181 million)

Business Opportunities

- Retail
- Industrial services and supplies for major projects

Commercial Real Estate

- Industrial parks are located right at the port and just outside Prince Rupert. Almost 1,000 hectares of land are available in the area for business opportunities.
- Prince Rupert is looking to redevelop and revitalize the town. Tax incentives include a Property Revitalization Tax Exemption and Facade Improvement Program.

Local Resources

- CFTKTV Terrace www.cftktv.com
- The Northern View www.thenorthernview.com
- Hecate Strait Employment Development Society hseds.ca

- North West Community College – Prince Rupert Campus
  www.nwcc.bc.ca
- University of Northern BC – Prince Rupert Campus
  www.unbc.ca/northwest

Unique Prince Rupert

In North America, Prince Rupert's port is the closest to Asia and the deepest natural ice-free harbour. With year-over-year growth of 13.8 per cent, it is also North America's fastest growing port.

Simon Fraser University is launching an Executive MBA program specifically tailored to Northwest British Columba. Classes will be taught in Prince Rupert and focus on key local industries: extractive resources, engineering, liquefied natural gas, and its related industries.

Northwest Coast, British Columbia

Northwest British Columbia – **Terrace**

Location: 1,356 km northwest of Vancouver, 110 minute flight

Population: 16,246 (2014 BC Stats, Census Agglomeration)

Key Industries: Business services, retail trade, health care, education, manufacturing

Overview

Built along the Skeena River, Terrace is known as the "Gateway to the North." The Northwest is experiencing a boom in natural gas, solid wood, and mining related activity. Terrace serves as a major commercial, transportation, and service hub for the region.

Business Organizations

- Terrace Economic Development Authority www.teda.ca
- Visit Terrace (Kermodei Tourism Society) www.visitterrace.com
- Terrace Chamber of Commerce www.terracechamber.com
- Community Futures www.1637cfdc.bc.ca

Aboriginal Peoples in the Region

- Kitselas www.kitselas.com
- Kitsumkalum www.kitsumkalum.bc.ca
- Nisga'a Lisims government www.nisgaanation.ca

Major Projects

Under construction in 2015

- Brucejack Mine, Pretium Resources ($665 million)
- Avanti Kitsault Mine, Alloycorp Mining Inc. Avanti Kitsault ($818 million)
- Skeena Industrial Development Park, City of Terrace/Kitselas First Nation ($100 million)

Proposed

- Galore Creek Mine, NovaGold, and Teck Resources ($4 billion)
- Geothermal Power Plant, Enbridge/Borealis Inc./Kitselas First Nation ($30 million)
- Kitimat Clean Oil Refinery, Kitimat Clean Ltd. ($19 billion)

Business Opportunities

- Four-star hotel, conference and convention center
- Restaurant—all levels
- Retail—all levels
- Office building

Transportation

- Airport, rail, passenger rail
- Highway 37, Yellowhead Highway16, Nisga'a Hwy

Commercial Real Estate

- The Skeena Industrial Development Park consists of 971 hectares of industrial land along Highway 37 adjacent to the Northwest Regional Airport.
- The City of Terrace and private owners have a combined 60 acres in the middle of town. The land is changing zoning from Heavy Industrial to Light Industrial, Core Commercial, and Multi-family Residential.

Local Resources

- Terrace Standard www.terracestandard.com
- Community Website www.terrace.ca
- Skeena Diversity Society www.skeenadiversity.com
- North West Community College www.nwcc.bc.ca
- University of Northern British Columbia www.unbc.ca

What happens if LNG Doesn't Go Ahead?

Alex Pietralla grew up in Central Europe and has lived in Terrace since 2009.

What economic opportunities do you see in Northern British Columbia?

I think it obviously hinges on big projects going ahead or not. The stability and growth and health of the communities will predominantly depend on the services that can then have sustainable growth and income from these large projects. The supply chain effects of a large LNG project are what's going to make these small communities live and thrive for a very long time. We tend to look at the initial investment, $10 billion, 15, 20. But those are spent over four to five years.

Communities need to think in decades. And what happens with these large investments is you're going to have small and medium businesses that are catering and servicing these sites. Once they're built, they're going to build communities; business people are going to have families here and they're going to create employment. There are many examples of these. It can be professionals like engineers, maintenance shops, pipe outfitters, security people – all kinds of services that can be outsourced outside the fences of these projects and make small business thrive.

What about when those large projects are completed?

When they're in operation, they still need services, they still need engineers, technicians, outside services that can do maintenance for them, or cleaning and so forth. I've seen some of the figures; for every direct job when in operation, let's say an LNG plant has 200 there will be 2 to 3.5 jobs outside of the operation.

Do you still see business opportunities if the large projects don't go ahead?

Yes I do. Terrace has a fair amount of health services that other communities of this size don't have because we are a hub for the region. We're a retail centre too. So anything that has to do with health services, retail, and tourism will always have a place here and be able to thrive.

Rio Tinto (smelter in Kitimat) is finishing their project this year so that gives the region sustainable growth because you have 1,000 jobs, which feeds 6,000 people in a community. And that's a base that Terrace and Kitimat can build on. And even if LNG doesn't go, the Northwest Transmission Line was built, so we have mining projects and we have the Port in Prince Rupert which is steadily growing.

CHAPTER 2
Aboriginal Peoples
Some Basics

It's astounding that it's taken a whole team of scientists and more than 150 years to figure out that our people weren't standing there with a frying pan …waiting for a (salmon) to jump in.

Kim Recalma-Clutesi, on archeological research showing coastal Aboriginal Peoples used sophisticated clam farming techniques[1]

When you are new to business in Northern British Columbia, it helps to appreciate the importance of Aboriginal Peoples' participation in the economy and to have a basic knowledge of their history and cultures. By understanding their role, you gain insights into the ways that potential resource projects might reduce their ability to exercise their rights and practice their cultures. Aboriginal Peoples have lived in the North for thousands of years. Prior to contact with Europeans, they had built continental trading networks that supported thriving communities on the Coast and in the Interior of what is now known as British Columbia.

Tip

People can sometimes become confused about the term "Aboriginal." It is similar to the term "North American." Individuals who live on the continent are called North Americans; you can be a North American, but you are also Canadian, American, or Mexican.

Some Definitions[2]

First, it's useful to be familiar with some basic terminology. **Aboriginal** is Canada's official name for the three distinct indigenous groups that are recognized under Section 35 of the *Canadian Constitution*. The section reads, "In this Act, *'aboriginal peoples of Canada'* includes the Indian, Inuit and Métis peoples of Canada." In the 2011 National Household Survey, prepared by Statistics Canada, 1,400,685 people self-identified as Aboriginal, representing 4.3 per cent of the total Canadian population.

Of the three Aboriginal groups mentioned in the Constitution, **First Nations** (which is the term most Canadians use today instead of "Indians," unless referring to specific legal matters) are descendants of the original inhabitants of Canada who lived here for thousands of years before explorers arrived from Europe. (The Europeans thought they had reached India and so called the inhabitants "Indians." That term has fallen out of general usage. Legal documents, however, as will be seen below, continue to use the formal, legal term, Indian.)

Today, First Nations people self-identify by the nation to which they belong; for example, Haida, Tahltan, Haisla, and so on. Over 600 Nations exist within Canada. Most Nations are made up of **bands** that have their own Chief and Council, land, and community. The majority of bands have fewer than 1,000 members. About half of First Nations individuals live on what are known as "reserve lands" or "reserves." A reserve is a tract of land, for which the federal government has title, set apart for the use and benefit of a band; there are about 2,300 in Canada. Some bands have more than one reserve. Individuals cannot own land on a reserve in Canada.

Inuit inhabit the Arctic regions of Canada, the United States, and Greenland. In Canada in 2011, 59,445 people self-identified as Inuit, about 0.2 per cent of the population. Very few Inuit live in British Columbia.

The Métis trace their roots and evolution to the fur trade, where it was common for European men to marry First Nation women. The Métis developed their own language (Michif), arts, music, and crafts. They have a distinct relationship with the Canadian government, since, unlike First Nations bands, they are not subject to the *Indian Act*. According to the 2011 Canadian census, 69,475 Métis people lived in British Columbia.

Aboriginal Peoples in Northern British Columbia

On the following page is a map of British Columbia, showing the different Aboriginal communities and their locations in Northern British Columbia. Around these communities, First Nations have identified traditional territories where their communities have exercised their rights for generations. Territory is often shared or overlaps with that of other First Nations bands. Administrative offices are located in or near the following places, which will give you an idea of which Aboriginal group you might be engaging or working with.

Table 2.1: Aboriginal Peoples

Location	Aboriginal Peoples in the Area
Haida Gwaii	Haida
Prince Rupert	Tsimshian First Nations, comprising five communities: Gitga'at, Kitasoo/Xai'xais, Kitselas, Kitsumkalum, and Metlakatla First Nations. This territory is bordered by the traditional lands of the Gitxsan, Nisga'a, and Haida.
Terrace	Kitselas and Kitsumkalum. Up the Nass Valley are the offices of the Nisga'a Lisims government.
Kitimat	Haisla
Hazelton	Gitxsan communities and Gitanyow
Smithers	Wet'suwet'en communities (5)
Burns Lake	Lake Babine and Ts'il Kaz Koh (Burns Lake Band)
Prince George	Lheidli T'enneh, Carrier Sekani Tribal Council (CSTC) (representing eight First Nations), McLeod Lake, Prince George Métis Community Association
Fort St. John	Doig River, Blueberry River, Halfway River, Métis Society
Dawson Creek	Saulteau, West Moberly, Métis Society
Fort Nelson	Fort Nelson, Prophet River Band

Figure 3: Map of Aboriginal Communities in Northern British Columbia

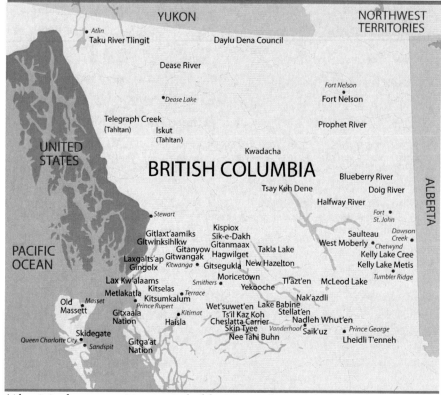

(Aboriginal communities are in bold, cities and towns in italics.)

Governance

Prior to European contact, some First Nations in British Columbia, particularly on the Northwest Coast, had developed governance structures that divided the people into clans or wilps, headed by hereditary chiefs. Clans were the primary unit for governance, decision-making, and jurisdiction over land and resources. Chiefs made decisions through consensus, after extensive consultation with families within the clan. Some Nations would continue to deliberate until they had addressed all objections, while others had fall-back mechanisms to reach a decision, such as intervention by traditional leaders. As leaders, hereditary chiefs were to ensure that the families for which they were responsible had a voice within the government. If a family's wishes were misrepresented or underrepresented, their sense of belonging and loyalty to their chief could be compromised.[3]

In 1876, this traditional governing process changed. The Canadian government passed the *Indian Act*, which gave the federal government exclusive authority to govern First Nations (Indian) people and their associated reserve lands. It addressed such issues as education, health care, and local government. The *Indian Act* also identified who could be given status as an Indian (the legal term) and how a person could lose this status. While the federal government has amended the Act many times, it remains a contentious document for many First Nations.

The purpose of the *Indian Act* was to assimilate First Nations into mainstream Canadian society. Each band is required to have a uniform governance structure whereas previously, as outlined above, hereditary chiefs and clans governed many communities in British Columbia. Under the *Indian Act*, First Nations must elect a Chief and Council, generally every two or three years. The hereditary system, however, remains a part of many First Nations, so you will sometimes meet both an elected and a hereditary chief (two different people) in a business meeting.

Some First Nations in British Columbia have also negotiated treaties or agreements in principle with the federal and/or provincial governments and are self-governing. In the Northeast, in 1899, eight Bands adhered to Treaty 8[4]: Blueberry River, Doig River, Fort Nelson, Halfway River, Prophet River, Saulteau, West Moberly, and McLeod Lake (which adhered in March 2000). It's important to note that these Nations made a treaty with the federal government, but not the provincial government. Under the British Columbia treaty process, which started in 1993 for communities not included in Treaty 8, each First Nation is negotiating or has negotiated a self-government arrangement to meet its unique social, cultural, political, and economic needs. In 1998, four Nisga'a communities negotiated the first modern-day treaty. Other mainly urban First Nations have also concluded treaties, but the majority has not. (More on the treaty process follows.)

The *Indian Act* excluded the Métis and Inuit. In 2014, the Canadian Federal Court of Appeal ruled that the Métis have the same rights as Status Indians under the Canadian Constitution and therefore should receive similar rights and benefits from the federal government. (The question of whether the provincial or federal governments were responsible for the Métis was disputed for many years.) The federal government appealed this decision, known as the Daniels case; the Supreme Court of Canada will hear the appeal in October of 2015.

The Métis Nation British Columbia is the governing nation for Métis people living in British Columbia and is a member of the Métis National Council. In addition to the Council, the British Columbia Métis Federation is a non-profit association that works with Métis communities to ensure the well-being of its members. The goal of these organizations is to implement self-government within the Canadian federation.

Some History: Aboriginal Trading Networks

Aboriginal Peoples have been living in what is now British Columbia for thousands of years - and trading throughout the area for the same amount of time. Archeologists first thought there had been inhabitants in the region for 10,000 years, but then found bone implements that suggests hunting peoples have lived in Northwest Canada for as many as 40,000 years. Many Aboriginal Peoples believe they have existed in particular locations since human beings first appeared on earth. Population estimates in British Columbia, before contact with Europeans, range from 80-200,000 people.[5]

In the Northeast, Aboriginal Peoples were organized into hunting groups, and moved throughout the region hunting buffalo, moose, elk, caribou, and deer. In the Northwest, people spent more time in large village sites. Food sources included sea mammals, shellfish, salmon, and berries, as well as moose, bear, and deer. They also maintained an expansive system of clam farms, using sophisticated cultivation techniques to intensify production.[6] In the Northwest, travel and trade corridors were centred on the Skeena and Nass Rivers and their tributaries. These corridors linked coastal First Nations with Interior groups via routes called "grease trails" because of the volume of prized eulachon fish grease transported along them.

Aboriginal Peoples established extensive North America-wide trade networks, held regular trade fairs, and exchanged a variety of commodities and other goods. Trade fairs were held at locations with exceptionally rich fisheries such as the mouth of the Nass River in Northwest British Columbia. These fairs drew thousands of visitors from far and wide, who exchanged foods as well as goods such as copper, moose hides, and slaves. On the coast, large ocean-going canoes carrying goods or people travelled hundreds of kilometres north and south.[7] (The excellent *Historical Atlas of Canada, Volume 1*, includes maps showing Aboriginal trade routes at the local, regional, and continental scales. Routes in the Pacific coast region were particularly abundant.)

Some First Nations established gateway communities that sometimes were fortified forts. They acted as middlemen between groups of producers and consumers, controlling trade through threat or force. In the Northwest, the national historical site at Fort Kitwanga is the location of what was an especially strategic crossroads in the trading trails.

Near Hazelton, British Columbia

Table 2.2: By the Numbers–Aboriginal Demographics and Social Indicators

232,290	In 2011, people identifying themselves as Aboriginal living in British Columbia, or about 5.4 per cent of the provincial population. Aboriginal is Canada's official name for the three distinct indigenous groups that are recognized in the Canadian Constitution: Indians (now generally known as First Nations), Métis, and Inuit.
155,020	Number of people self-identifying as First Nations in British Columbia in 2011.
69,475	Number of people self-identifying as Métis in British Columbia in 2011.
34	Number of First Nations languages and associated cultures in British Columbia.
203	Number of bands in British Columbia.
21	Tribal associations that represent Aboriginal collectives in British Columbia.
8	Number of treaties or agreements in principle signed with BC First Nations since 1993.
$22,344	Median income of an Aboriginal person in 2011, 60 per cent of the Canadian average.
35	Drinking Water Advisories in effect in 31 BC First Nations communities in 2014.
1,400	National incarceration (prison) rate per 100,000 population, 10 times the national rate.
50	Percentage of children in the care of the provincial government who were Aboriginal, in 2014.
61.6	Percentage of Aboriginal students in British Columbia who graduated from high school in six years in 2013-14. Completion rate for the whole province was 84.2 per cent.
26	Median age of First Nations people in Canada in 2011. The median age for the overall Canadian population was 42 years.

The Arrival of the Fur Traders

First contacts between Aboriginal people and Europeans in British Columbia came largely through the fur trade. In the Northwest, Russian explorers and traders were moving into the Aleutians and one expedition in 1741 reached the coast near Cross Sound (on the present-day Alaska Panhandle). In 1774, a

Spanish vessel headed north from Mexico to explore the coastline and trade. It reached the vicinity of Haida Gwaii and then sailed to Northern Vancouver Island. In 1775, two more Spanish ships reached as far north as the Alaska coast. The British followed with two ships in 1778 and reached the west coast of Vancouver Island. The Europeans spent a month with the First Nations people there, refitting their ships and trading for sea otter furs. Once the ships reached China, the price these furs fetched made further trading voyages an appealing and lucrative prospect to many Europeans and Americans.

The race was on! As soon as this news spread, trading ships from the United States, England, France, and Spain flocked to the Northwest coast. They traded goods with the Aboriginal people for furs, which they took to China, obtaining new cargo for the voyage home. The peak years of this trade on the coast were between 1792 and 1812, before the sea otter largely disappeared from over-hunting.

Meanwhile, European fur traders came by land to the Northeast, as part of a slow progression that had started on Canada's East Coast. In 1778, Aboriginal guides took explorer Peter Pond to Methye Portage, opening up another route into Canada's prime trapping and hunting grounds. In 1793, with the help of Aboriginal guides, Alexander Mackenzie travelled up the Peace River and then continued by river to the west coast (although the last part was by land, along a well-known "grease trail.") Without Aboriginal labour, translation skills, and knowledge of the land, the explorers would have likely perished on their journeys, never finding the routes they sought. Other explorers followed and by 1805 Europeans had established fur-trading posts at Fort Nelson, Fort St. John, and Hudson's Hope, to name a few.

Aboriginal Peoples were experts in trading and bartering where furs were another item often exchanged. Initially, they trapped and delivered the furs to trading posts to bargain with Europeans for goods and supplies. They were by no means passive recipients of whatever trinkets the traders chose to offer; they held out for goods they wanted and drove hard bargains.[8]

In fact, certain groups became middlemen, buying furs from other groups and re-selling them to European traders with an appropriate mark-up. The Tsimshian, for example, took control of all the trade along the Skeena and Stikine rivers. Once, a Tlingit chief led a war party inland and wiped out a small Hudson's Bay post that threatened his trade monopoly. Soon, the European and American traders learned it was wiser to co-operate with the local Aboriginal people rather than to try to compete with them.

In its day, the fur trade was the biggest commercial enterprise in North America and British Columbia, then a colony, was its final epicentre, with trading forts springing up on many rivers and lakes. The industry maintained a transportation system that both knit the colony together and tied it to the rest of Canada.

A First Nations Perspective on the Fur Traders

Chief and Dr. Joseph Gosnell, Chief Negotiator for the Nisga'a on the Nisga'a Treaty, speaking to the British Columbia Legislature December 2, 1998.[9]

Our first encounters with Europeans were friendly. We welcomed these strange visitors—visitors who never left. The Europeans also valued their encounters with us. They thought we were fair and tough entrepreneurs and—no doubt today—negotiators. In 1832 traders from the Hudson's Bay Co. found our people living, in their words, 'in two-storey wooden houses the equal of any in Europe.' For a time our people prospered, but there were dark days yet to come.

By the late 1850s, as increasing numbers of settlers arrived (many drawn by the Cariboo Gold Rush in the Interior of BC), Aboriginal communities began a long period of social and economic decline. European government structures became formalized. The earlier commerce-based relationships were replaced by legislation such as the Indian Act of 1876, which took control of Aboriginal community governance. Further, the introduction of firearms, diseases like smallpox, and alcohol devastated Aboriginal communities. Thousands died. (The Nisga'a population, for example, decreased from thousands to 800 through the 1800s.[10]) Community members who survived were herded onto reservations, lost their rights, and were subject to a series of laws and measures from the federal government, designed to assimilate them into broader Canadian society.

Aboriginal Education and Residential Schools

The federal government's residential school policies had a largely negative impact on Aboriginal Peoples.[11] Though the schools are now closed, the effects of them still haunt communities, families, and individuals today. In fact, when you meet an older Aboriginal person, a high likelihood exists that he or she once attended a residential school; often, former students refer to themselves as "survivors."

In 1831, before Canada became a nation, Aboriginal children began to be educated in residential schools. In 1883, the Canadian government developed a policy of using residential schools as a primary means to "civilize" and "assimilate" Aboriginal Peoples. Working with various churches, it established a network of 132 residential schools across Canada, with some remaining in operation until 1996. In these schools, Aboriginal youngsters were to be educated in the same manner and on the same subjects as other Canadian children. These institutions forced them to abandon their traditional languages, dress, religion, and lifestyles. As Chief Justice Beverley McLachlin said in 2015, it was "cultural genocide."

As the years passed and when Aboriginal Peoples took charge of educating their children, the legacy of the residential school system became increasingly apparent. Stories surfaced about school administrators and teachers abusing, mistreating, and assaulting children, who often lived in deplorable conditions with limited food. Over 6,000 died. As residential school survivor Gilbert Oskaboose wrote in 1993:

> Human beings of any race generally learn their behaviours through observing their parents, peers, and role models. Whatever happened to Indian children where the natural process was broken? What happened to Indian children who were taken away at a young age – four or five years - and raised in alien hostile environments, completely separated from their parents, peer groups, language, culture, role models, familiar surroundings...?
>
> How do such children get to learn the history of their own people when it was viewed through the biased account of another culture? ...What happened to the parents who were forced to stand by and watch their children being taken away from them?... What happened to their relationships that normally exist between them and their children?...

When the residential schools were finished with their "education" thousands of children returned to hundreds of different villages, minus their language, ignorant of their cultures... lost between two different worlds.[12]

As claims and litigation against the federal government and churches increased, the first steps toward reconciliation began in the 1990s. Various churches offered their apologies to residential school survivors and in 1998, the government also acknowledged its role.

The impact of Indian Residential Schools continues even today. In its final report in 1996, the Royal Commission on Aboriginal Peoples noted the deep and lasting negative impact this policy had on children who attended the residential schools, as well as their families, communities, and cultures.[13] Residential schools directly contributed to the social problems that exist today, through the loss of cultural identity and traditional ways of life. Their legacy, along with inadequate health care, sub-standard housing, and high levels of unemployment plague many Aboriginal communities in British Columbia.

Further, from the 1960s to the 1980s, child-welfare services across Canada took thousands of Aboriginal children from their homes and placed them with non-Aboriginal families, some in the United States (the "Sixties Scoop"). Many Aboriginal Peoples consider the adoptions as an extension of residential schools. In 2015, some adoptees sued the federal government for the emotional trauma and loss of their culture.[14]

In 2007, in response to Canada's largest class action lawsuit, the Canadian government announced a landmark compensation package for residential school survivors, worth nearly $2 billion. In 2008, in the House of Commons, Prime Minster Stephen Harper offered a full apology on behalf of Canadians for the system. As he stated:

For more than a century, Indian Residential Schools separated over 150,000 Aboriginal children from their families and communities. In the 1870's, the federal government, partly...to meet its obligation to educate Aboriginal children, began to play a role in the development and administration of these schools.

Two primary objectives of the Residential Schools system were to remove and isolate children from the influence of their homes, families, traditions, and cultures, and to assimilate them into the dominant culture. These objectives were based on the assumption Aboriginal cultures and spiritual beliefs were inferior and unequal. Indeed, some sought, as it was infamously said, "to kill the Indian in the child"...[15]

The federal government also established the Indian Residential Schools Truth and Reconciliation Commission (TRC) which carried on activities across Canada from 2008 until June 2015. The Commission had the responsibility of:

• Telling Canadians what happened in the Indian Residential Schools

• Honouring the lives of former students and their families

• Creating a permanent record of the Indian Residential School legacy

Local Knowledge: Highway of Tears

The Highway of Tears is the local name for an 800 kilometer section of Highway 16, between Prince George and Prince Rupert, British Columbia. Between 1969 and 2011, more than 18 women, over half Aboriginal, were murdered or disappeared along the route, according to police. Aboriginal organizations estimate that over 40 women are missing, because they include women who disappeared a greater distance from the highway.

Between 1980 and 2012, 1,017 Aboriginal women were victims of homicide which represents roughly 16 per cent of all female homicides— far greater than their representation in Canada's female population.[16]

As part of their activities, the TRC met with and collected the experiences of former students, staff, their families, and anyone else that had an experience to share. The Commission held major events and hearings, including a National Event in Vancouver in September 2013. In preparation, the TRC held public hearings in northern communities such as Prince George, Williams Lake, and Terrace. Residential school survivors from these and adjacent communities shared their experiences with the Commission in public and private sessions.

Aboriginal Peoples in British Columbia
A Legal and Policy Context You Need to Know

As a business person, you may have limited interest in history, government policies and the ongoing legal wrangling that takes place between the federal and provincial governments and Aboriginal Peoples. This history and these court cases and policies, however, have an enormous impact on business, either directly, if you're in the resource sector, or indirectly, in terms of overall economic activity in the North. To summarize it briefly, Aboriginal Peoples may have had some losses in the legislature, but they have a consistent record of winning in court.

What is key to comprehend is that in British Columbia, the colonial government stopped negotiating treaties with First Nations in the mid-1800s. In the 20th century, Nations turned instead to the courts to assert their rights. Today, as the result of a series of legal victories beginning in 1973, governments now recognize Aboriginal title, but the two parties are still working out the full ramifications and implementation measures.

Negotiating Title/Resolving Land Claims

Dozens of books on the history of land claims and the treaty process in British Columbia are available (see the Bibliography for examples). What follows is a summary of some of the more pertinent dates, activities, and court cases in the land claims/treaty saga.

- **1763: The Royal Proclamation**—In 1763, Britain became the primary European power throughout much of North America, controlling most of the commercial fur trade. King George III issued a Royal Proclamation in 1763, which established strict protocols for all dealings with First Nations. The Proclamation was designed to solve the problem of private transfers of Aboriginal land. It decreed that individual settlers could not buy this land: instead, Aboriginal land was to be surrendered to the Crown through a treaty process. In short, British colonial policy recognized that Aboriginal groups were sovereign nations whose title to the land was recognized by English law and international law.

- **1854: Colonial government stops negotiating treaties**—In British Columbia, unlike the rest of Canada, the colonial government negotiated only a handful of treaties with First Nations, mostly on Vancouver Island. Treaty making stopped after 1854 because of British Columbia's reluctance to recognize Indian land rights. Contrary to international and British law (as well as Canadian policy), the government of British Columbia took possession of most of its lands without entering into treaties.

- **1899: Treaty 8 signed**—In the Northeast, certain First Nations negotiated Treaty 8 with Canada in 1899. The Western boundary of this Treaty, however, remains in dispute, and as of 2015, a case to determine its location was before the British Columbia Supreme Court.

  As well, in April 2015, three of the First Nations which signed the Treaty (Prophet River First Nation, West Moberly First Nations, and the McLeod Lake Indian Band) were in court, arguing that the creation of a large hydroelectric dam in their region ("Site C") violated their rights under Treaty 8.[17] Around the same time, the Blueberry River First Nations launched a civil claim in the BC Supreme Court that challenges the cumulative impacts of industrial development in its traditional territory. The Nation alleges that years of development, including mining, forestry, and oil and gas projects, and the proposed Site C, have violated its treaty rights under Treaty 8.

- **1973: The Calder Case**—The Nisga'a First Nation from Northwest British Columbia successfully sued the Government of British Columbia in the Supreme Court of Canada. The Court ruled that modern Canadian law recognizes Aboriginal rights to land based on historic occupation and possession. The case provided the foundation for the first modern treaty in British Columbia, the Nisga'a Final Agreement (which came into effect in May 2000), and for the British Columbia treaty process to be started after 130 years of opposition by colonial and later provincial authorities.

- **1990: The Sparrow Case**—The Supreme Court of Canada clarifies constitutionally protected Aboriginal fishing rights. In addition, it rules that Aboriginal and treaty rights are capable of evolving over time and governments must interpret them generously. The Court also confirms that these rights are not absolute, and governments can infringe upon them providing they can legally justify it.

- **1992: Treaty process restarts**—British Columbia, Canada, and First Nations re-started the treaty process. In 2015, after 23 years of negotiations, a total of eight treaties or agreements in principle were signed. Costs for the process, as of 2014, were over 600 million dollars.

Tip

The Union of BC Indian Chiefs (www.ubcic.bc.ca) offers an online timeline of events and court cases related to Aboriginal Peoples from the 1700s to 2010. As well, the University of British Columbia's Indigenous Foundations website (indigenousfoundations.arts.ubc.ca) offers rich and detailed information on court cases, events, and government policies.

- **1984-1997: The Delgamuukw Case**—In a landmark ruling, after years of trials, the Supreme Court of Canada confirmed the existence of Aboriginal Title. It noted that Aboriginal Title is not a right of absolute ownership, but a proprietary right to "exclusive use and occupation of land" that "is a burden on the Crown's underlying title." Once Aboriginal Title is proven, federal and provincial governments may infringe upon it for valid reasons, including resource extraction, economic and infrastructure development, settlement of foreign populations and environmental protection. Aboriginal people must be consulted and compensated for any infringement or extinguishment of Aboriginal Title.

2004: Non-treaty negotiations start

With the slow pace of the expensive formal treaty process, many First Nations started looking for a faster way to move ahead. Instead of years at a Treaty

Negotiation table, they negotiated bilateral non-treaty agreements with the BC government, sometimes referred to as "incremental treaty agreements." (Note that the Government of Canada is not part of this process.) The British Columbia government shares provincial tax revenue from mining, forestry, and other resources with First Nations, with shares ranging from 12.5 to 37.5 per cent of what the province collects. In 2014, the provincial government signed a mineral tax agreement with the Nisga'a Nation that provide it with an estimated $43 million in tax revenues over the projected 16 year life of the planned Avanti Kitsault molybdenum mine. In 2015, it was negotiating an agreement with Tahltan Nation for a mineral tax agreement on the Red Chris mine.

From 2013 to 2015, British Columbia signed 16 incremental treaty agreements that transfer provincial Crown land so that Aboriginal communities can take action on economic and community development opportunities. It has provided tens of millions of dollars to allow First Nations to obtain equity stakes in clean energy and pipeline developments. It has reached a series of reconciliation framework agreements that include decision-making, revenue-sharing, economic, and social-development elements. In total, the province has reached more than 300 economic development agreements with First Nations that did not involve the federal government or treaties.[18]

2014 Game Changer: The William Case (Tsilhqot'in First Nation)

In 2014, after 24 years of litigation, the Supreme Court of Canada ruled in favour of the Tsilhqot'in First Nation (near Williams Lake, British Columbia) deciding that the Nation holds title to 1,750 square kilometres of land in BC's Chilcotin region. The decision means that anyone wanting to use those lands must first obtain permission from the Tsilhqot'in. As noted in *Business in Vancouver*[19]:

> The Tsilhqot'in (decision) represents the first time in Canadian history that Aboriginal title has been granted outside an Indian reserve and can extend to all traditional territories (which can be thousands of square kilometres in size). This is particularly important in BC, where outstanding land claims cover more than 100% of the province's lands (due to overlapping claims).

Even more important, the judgment states that once Aboriginal title has been recognized, project development requires the consent of the First Nation that holds title, except where the government can demonstrate a compelling and substantial public purpose for the project. In addition, decisions will be retroactive.

The court decision also states: "If the Crown begins a project without consent prior to Aboriginal title being established, it may be required to cancel the project upon establishment of the title."

The high court underscored that Aboriginal title has to be taken seriously wherever it is asserted, meaning it should be met by methodical analysis, meaningful consultation, and substantial accommodation to minimize impacts. In short, resource developments in British Columbia must now operate with the knowledge that the consent of Aboriginal communities is a requirement for future use of that land. At the same time, where lands have been identified and validated for a single First Nation community, resource developers will have certainty as to whom they will need to consult and accommodate.

In the case of Tsilhqot'in, in March 2015, they enacted the *Affirmation of the Nemiah Declaration*. The *Declaration* states there shall be no commercial logging, no "mining or mining explorations," "no commercial road building," and "no dam construction." If any non-Aboriginals want to use the Nemiah Aboriginal Wilderness Preserve that the Tsilhqot'in created, they can only do so with the Nation's permission, through a system of permits. Visitors with the proper permits can hunt, fish, canoe, and engage in light camping.[20]

2015 Game Changer: Eyford Report on the Treaty Process in Canada

Two potentially major changes to the treaty-making environment occurred in 2015. First, in March, the provincial government withdrew its support for a new head of the British Columbia Treaty Commission. (First Nations and the federal government had approved the new commissioner.) The government then said it would not support any candidate to serve as Chief Commissioner, and the Premier questioned whether the Treaty Commission should even exist.

In April 2015, the report *A New Direction: Advancing Aboriginal and Treaty Rights* was released. The federal government had commissioned its author, lawyer Douglas Eyford, to examine the treaty process and make recommendations. Eyford was blunt.

> Modern treaty negotiations in British Columbia began in 1993. At the time, it was anticipated that treaty-making would be completed by 2000.
>
> After more than 20 years of negotiations, it is clear those expectations were overly ambitious if not unrealistic. Still, important lessons have been learned. Only four treaties have been concluded under the BC treaty process. Today, 53 tables representing approximately half of the Indian Act bands in the province are engaged in the process. Only four tables are at the stage of negotiating a final agreement. While predicting outcomes in treaty negotiations is challenging, it is improbable that each of the 53 tables will complete a final agreement. It is more likely that no more than ten tables are likely to conclude a treaty in the foreseeable future.[21]

Eyford suggests that talks be abandoned where there is little or no hope of success. Further, he said modern treaties aren't "realistic" for many Canadian Aboriginal groups, and urged Canada to reach agreements much like the economic and resource development agreements that the British Columbia government had been negotiating with First Nations (mentioned in a previous section).

The Bottom Line

So, where do all these court cases, reports and policies leave us? Basically, a succession of Supreme Court of Canada decisions have refined and clarified the rights of Aboriginal Peoples under section 35 of the *Canadian Constitution*. In the eyes of many, it is not a formalized treaty or title rights that influence business relations with First Nations today; it is the negotiating power they have that is conferred by the Court's ruling and the legal recognition of the duty of senior governments to consult and accommodate.

In fact, by 2015, the most important negotiations in British Columbia between government and First Nations may be taking place through economic and resource development agreements. In many cases, both sides want to move on from litigation and treaty talks. This is not to say, however, that either process is going away, but now, an alternative exists, and many First Nations are using it, with willingness on the part of the provincial government as well.

As this chapter demonstrates, the ongoing negotiations and lawsuits between the provincial and federal governments and Aboriginal Peoples make for a complex and often confusing and perplexing environment for the private sector. Nonetheless, business and Aboriginal groups are working together and many First Nations are actively engaged in community economic development and starting private businesses. The next chapter outlines these activities and examines ways your company can get involved. There are many business opportunities with Aboriginal Peoples in the North if you're willing to be flexible, patient, and innovative.

CHAPTER 3
Doing Business with Aboriginal Peoples Today

Today, as a wise Chief in BC said to me…"Economic Development
is how we hunt today." If you call yourself a leader, give all your
people a chance at the dignity of a job, equal opportunity
and the individual responsibility to earn a living.[1]

Chief Clarence Louie

This chapter will help businesses seeking to develop relationships with Aboriginal communities and businesses. If you're planning to sell goods and services to major projects in the North, it's helpful to know that most project proponents will give preference to businesses that work with First Nation enterprises, either through subcontracts, joint venture partnerships, or other arrangements. As well, it will be useful for companies in any sector, since in Northern British Columbia, Aboriginal Peoples potentially represent a major source of employees and customers.

Some Basics on Aboriginal Business

Aboriginal people in Northern British Columbia face certain issues related to economic development:

1. They need to diversify beyond the fishing and forestry sectors when participating in the wage economy.

2. Some communities are receiving millions of dollars as a result of revenue sharing agreements and by performing contracting and supply services in support of resource development projects. In early 2015, 296 economic cooperation and revenue sharing agreements existed between First Nations and either government or corporations, according to the First Nations Economic Development Database (www.fnedd.ca/about.html). Some of these agreements have enabled the BC government to settle land claims without signing treaties.

Access to funding has allowed some First Nations to break out of a longstanding development trap. With money to build updated roads, water systems, and telecommunications networks, the communities can attract and support new business ventures and become more active in the regional economy. Essentially what is happening now is that some First Nations are balancing and leveraging infringements on their Aboriginal rights and title in exchange for economic benefits.

An Aboriginal business is defined as:

- A sole proprietorship owned and operated by a Status Indian, non-Status Indian, Métis, or Inuit person(s); or

- A limited company, a co-operative, a partnership, or a not-for-profit organization in which Aboriginal persons have at least 51 per cent ownership

- A joint venture consisting of two or more Aboriginal businesses or an Aboriginal business and a non-Aboriginal business(es), provided that the Aboriginal business(es) has at least 51 per cent ownership.

Source: BC Aboriginal Business Association
(www.bcaba.ca/aboriginal-business-certification)

These shifting circumstances are leading to the establishment of more Nation and individual-owned business enterprises (though not all communities support the individual approach). Some businesses in British Columbia and certain First Nation leaders are attempting to nurture what they say is a growing entrepreneurial spirit. Many resource developers, however, prefer to see economic benefits shared amongst the greatest number of people and so have greater interest in awarding larger contracts with Nation/community-owned business enterprises, joint venture relationships, or partnerships.

In a 2012 report, the TD Bank estimated that the total pre-tax income of Aboriginal households, businesses, and governments in Canada will be $32 billion by 2016. This amount would be larger than the combined economies of the provinces of Newfoundland and Prince Edward Island. BC has about 17 per cent of the Canadian Aboriginal population, so should see about $6 - $7 billion in total income by 2016.

The fastest growing part of this income projection comes from Aboriginal businesses. According to the TD Bank, 40 per cent of Aboriginal pre-tax income comes from business. It is estimated that in 2016, businesses will grow faster and be more significant than transfers from federal and provincial/territorial governments.

Aboriginal people are establishing businesses in a wide range of sectors, from forestry, fishing, and construction to arts and entertainment, technology, and corporate management. The form of these businesses includes increasing numbers of well-financed, Nation-run development corporations. Numerous First Nations in Northern BC have established an economic development corporation (EDC), with a focus to maximize and balance the prospects of a proposed development project with the priorities, interests, and needs of the community. Part of their work includes assessing whether a project is economically viable, socially responsible, and environmentally sustainable. Often First Nations will establish joint-ventures or limited partnerships with other business enterprises to have the capacity to pursue and win contracts. Below are some examples of business partnerships developed in recent years (with new partnerships and developments taking place on an ongoing basis).

- **Metlakatla First Nation** near Prince Rupert is striking deals to build port infrastructure. Its economic development corporation owns a shellfish hatchery facility and farms. It has partnered with Williams Moving and Storage and Island Tug and Barge and provides trucking and marine shipping services for the North Coast of BC.

- **Lax Kw'alaams Band** revenues in 2014 were over $56 million, with over $26 million coming from the 100 per cent band-owned forestry and logging company, Coast Tsimshian Resources (CTR). Brinkman Forest Ltd. manages the firm on behalf of the band. CTR is active in the Chinese market and has an office in Beijing. In 2014, CTR opened a new sawmill in Terrace with a Chinese partner and was partnering with Pinnacle Renewable Resources to build a wood pellet plant. The Band also owns an engineering firm and fish processing facility, among other businesses.

Northeastern British Columbia

- The **Nisga'a Lisims Government** and TransCanada signed a Benefits Agreement in 2014 that will allow almost 100 kilometres of a proposed natural gas pipeline to run through Nisga'a Lands. The Nation also has sites available for floating or land-based liquefied natural gas (LNG) facilities. Previously, the Nation had worked with BC Hydro on the development of the western alignment of the Northwest Transmission Line.

- The **Kitselas First Nation** near Terrace is forging natural gas pipeline agreements. With the City of Terrace as a partner, the Nation has set up Skeena Industrial Park which serves as a service and supply centre for the Northwest and a flagship for the city's economic development strategy. The Kitselas have leased 88 acres to Chevron for pipeline work.

- Kitimat is the proposed site for major liquefied natural gas (LNG) plants. The **Haisla First Nation** has 20 joint ventures or limited partnerships, in sectors ranging from light construction (Progressive Ventures), camp operations (ESS), camp construction (ATCO), environmental services (Triton), and others. The Nation owns an industry-focused training institute, Kitimat Valley Institute, with LNG Canada and Rio Tinto Alcan as partners.

- Fifteen to twenty mines are currently under consideration in **Tahltan** traditional territory. Red Chris, a major open pit copper-gold mine, opened in 2015. In addition, the Nation has been active with BC Hydro on the development of the Northwest Transmission Line and with Alta-Gas for Forest-Kerr and other run of the river (alternative energy) projects. The Nation has a joint venture with Rescan Environmental consultants.

- In 1987, **McLeod Lake** established Duz Cho Logging. It has grown to be one of British Columbia's largest logging companies with revenues of $70 million in 2014. Duz Cho Logging has diversified into the gas, oil, and mining sectors while maintaining the core harvesting operations. In August 2014, it established Duz Cho

Forest Products, exporting lumber from its outdoor sawmill to China, Japan, and the Middle East.

- **The Fort Nelson First Nation** owns 50 per cent of a drilling rig with Ensign Drilling and partners with Northwestel. It formed a joint-venture, Black Diamond Dene Limited Partnership, to build and provide accommodation and workspace camps for the energy industry in the Northeast. The Nation has also signed benefits agreements with TransCanada Pipeline and Spectra Energy.

Led by the growing revenue base of economic development corporations, the total income of Aboriginal businesses grew from an estimated $4 billion in 2001 to about $9 billion in 2011[2].

Economic activities go beyond the borders of Canada. The British Columbia First Nations Energy and Mining Council (FNEMC) developed the *First Nations-China Strategy* to promote a proactive approach to engagement with China. Numerous Chinese private companies and state-owned enterprises are approaching First Nations communities, interested in gaining access to their traditional territories. In 2015, FNEMC released another strategy for doing business with Japan. Firms from this nation are pursuing investments to export liquefied natural gas (LNG) and heavy rare earth elements, many which are on the traditional territories of First Nations.

Private Sector Aboriginal Businesses

In 2012, TD Bank estimated that only one-tenth of Aboriginal business income came from independent small business; the rest came from band-run economic development corporations. Nonetheless, more private Aboriginal companies are being established.[3]

The TD Report estimated that in 2007 there were 7,000 Aboriginal-owned businesses in BC. The First Nations Economic Development Database (www.fnedd.ca/about.html) launched in January 2015, lists over 1,000 businesses, in professional, scientific and technical services, construction, arts, entertainment and recreation, corporate management, retail, fishing and forestry, and accommodation and food services.

The numbers of small businesses are growing at a rate that is six times faster than in the non-Aboriginal market and Aboriginal entrepreneurs tend to be about 10 years younger than their non-Aboriginal counterparts. This growth is in some ways unsurprising since nearly half of Canada's Aboriginal population of about 1.4 million is under the age of 25. "There is a growing business culture in First Nations communities that can be further cultivated and built upon," the Business Council of British Columbia stated in 2014.[4]

Long time Entrepreneurs

An Aboriginal interviewee quoted in Entrepreneurship and indigenous identity, a study of identity work by indigenous entrepreneurs in British Columbia.[5]

I think Aboriginal entrepreneurship was always there. It's just that the word wasn't recognized as such back in the day. Because of a lot of our people did trade, you know. The Interior Salish with the Coast Salish and from Vancouver to Haida Gwaii. The trade was always there… It's just that it wasn't labeled, but now…white society is actually recognizing that First Nations can be entrepreneurs. Where they have always been before. But this time, it's with money, whereas back in the day it was with food or clothing.

With on-reserve businesses sprouting up and a largely young and increasingly urban Aboriginal population in Canada, the opportunities are sometimes compared to those offered by the emerging international markets like China and India—offering early-mover companies in some sectors the same kind of rapid and auspicious growth potential.

In the words of Clint Davis, vice-president of Aboriginal banking at TD Bank, "You'll hear Aboriginal leaders across the country say that, on the business side, we're probably about 20 years behind the rest of the country… So it isn't at its infancy but it's certainly at early stages."[6] There is vast potential for non-Aboriginal businesses to partner with interested Aboriginal firms and grow with them.

An Aboriginal Social Enterprise[7]

Aboriginal Travel Services (ATS) (www.aboriginaltravelservices.com) is BC's First Aboriginal-owned travel agency, focusing on business and leisure needs of companies, First Nations bands, and individual tourists.

"ATS is employing First Nations individuals that have local knowledge of authentic Aboriginal experiences and are able to tailor packages to a specific guest requirement," says Scott Roberts, vice-president. "We will also be selling market-ready product developed by Aboriginal Tourism BC on a consultancy basis currently and online in the future."

The agency was also developed as a social enterprise, with the dual purpose of selling travel services that "directly impact the culture and economic opportunities among First Nations communities we service," says Scott. "First Nations employment both within the agency and among the Aboriginal Tourism experiences we are selling is a key component of our business model."

ATS will also reinvest profits into the Aboriginal communities and tourism initiatives.

Plugging into Aboriginal Business Networks

As the previous section discussed, Aboriginal people, whether through Band corporations or private enterprise, are entering into partnerships, joint ventures, and other arrangements with non-Aboriginal firms. If you're interested in doing business with Aboriginal people, where do you start? If you have limited background/knowledge/experience, begin by enhancing your fundamental knowledge and understanding of their history, culture, and business practices. Here are a few options to consider:

- **Read**—Books like *First Nations 101* by Lynda Gray or *Working Effectively with Aboriginal Peoples*® by Robert and Cynthia Joseph offer a good overview of the basics. These authors are members of British Columbia First Nations, so address issues important in the province. Calvin Helin, another First Nations author from the Northwest, has written the informative *Dances with Dependency,* which explores Aboriginal economic history and advocates strategies to end poverty. Online sources like *Indigenous Business and Finance Today* (ibftoday.ca) provide news on the latest in

Aboriginal business and finance. *Nation Talk* (nationtalk.ca) offers a daily roundup of Aboriginal news from mainstream and Aboriginal media.

- **Contact associations**—Try talking to organizations like the Industry Council for Aboriginal Business or the Aboriginal Business and Investment Council. Métis Nation British Columbia (www.mnbc.ca) and the BC Métis Federation (bcmetis.com) both have online business directories. The Canadian Council for Aboriginal Business puts on seminars and sessions on hot topics in Vancouver. The Okwaho Network (www.okwahonetwork.com) connects "Indigenous business people with each other and with non-Indigenous people who want to work with Indigenous communities and businesses."

- **Get specialized training**—Bob Joseph of Indigenous Corporate Training (www.ictinc.ca) offers excellent one and two day workshops on the basics of engaging and working with Aboriginal people. I've taken his course and found it engaging, content-rich, and a great way to get up to speed.

- **Attend conferences**—Many organizations are holding conferences to enable Aboriginal and non-Aboriginal businesses to meet and explore opportunities. The *National Aboriginal Business Opportunities Conference* is held annually in Prince Rupert with a "focus on creating a comfortable and supportive venue for collaboration between Aboriginal and Private Sector business groups." *Aboriginal Business Match West* connects Aboriginal communities in BC and Alberta with the private sector to create opportunities for business. The Vancouver Board of Trade offers an annual *Aboriginal Opportunities Forum*. Conferences like the annual *B.C. Northeast Natural Gas Summit* (held in Vancouver) also frequently feature speakers addressing Aboriginal issues.

After developing some fundamental background knowledge, consider more direct contact with the appropriate First Nation(s). Here are some suggestions for this step:

- **Draw on the expertise of larger contractor firms**—If you're working as a supplier on a major project, resource developers or project proponents have extensive resources available to them. Developers who understand the impact of their projects on Aboriginal and Treaty rights can also provide guidance. Remember, though, that all resource development project teams or their corporations have their own values, drivers, and methods by which they manage their commitments to communities. These differences influence the success that they will have in fostering or hindering their relationships with Aboriginal Peoples.

- **Hire a consultant specializing in Aboriginal relationships**—Ask for referrals from your colleagues, a Chamber of Commerce, or economic development office, or search on-line for appropriate contacts. Engage an individual or firm that specializes in British Columbian Aboriginal relations or has a solid base of experience working with Aboriginal communities and businesses in Canada. Some larger consulting firms also have specialists in this area, related to engagement, relationship building, business and human capacity building, employment, contracting, and negotiations.

- **Get legal advice**—An understanding of Aboriginal rights and title and recent law is helpful. If your project is substantial, find a lawyer familiar with Aboriginal law and issues in BC (and ask around, since some are great and others not), preferably with experience drafting agreements between and among First Nation businesses and others. It's valuable for both parties to get legal advice to ensure the terms of the agreement are tailored to the situation, and meet both parties needs.

- **Go direct**—Here's a suggested list of steps, compiled for the Resort Developers of BC, but applicable in many other sectors as well.

  1. Check the community's website or the Aboriginal Affairs and Northern Development Canada website (Community Profiles section) for updated information on the names of the current Chief and Council.

2. Contact the community and confirm the contact information, address, and so forth.

3. If the Nation has a business or economic development office, call to ask for advice on how to proceed: each Nation or community will have different processes to explore and discuss opportunities.

4. Send a letter of introduction to the current elected Chief and Council requesting a meeting with the Chief or designated Council member and state the reasons for the meeting. You may also send a copy of the letter to the First Nation's Administrator and/or Economic/Business Development department, if there is one.

5. Follow up with a telephone call after one to two weeks to confirm receipt of your correspondence and to schedule a meeting. It may be necessary to call a few more times and resend the correspondence.

Doing Business with First Nations on Resource Projects

Murray Slezak, retired Shell Canada Social Performance Team Leader
murray.slezak@shaw.ca

For over a decade, I have observed that when Aboriginal businesses receive a "helping hand" versus a "hand-out," they are generally more successful because of the encouragement and support of energy companies and their contractors. This is based on personal experiences, observing other corporations and contractors, and becoming familiar with case studies of global best practices. Capacity building is not limited to holding a one day workshop or seminar to tell Aboriginal community leaders, development corporations, and entrepreneurs of the potential opportunities and pre-qualification requirements. If that is all that happens, there will be no sustainable businesses to support projects and operations. Frustration will grow and expectations will not be fulfilled. Assisting businesses to be pre-qualified, identifying contract opportunities for single source negotiation, and being included on bid lists as well as ongoing coaching and support during the performance of the contract will lead to sustainable success.

When meaningful guidance and space is created for Aboriginal businesses to compete and participate in resource development activities, they experience sustainable growth. Their capabilities and capacities improve while developing a competitive value proposition for their customers. I prefer to work with Aboriginal businesses that are community owned as they generally employ the greatest number of community members and offer the broadest community benefit. There are many promoters of joint venture partnerships; however, not all Aboriginal businesses require a joint venture partner nor are they always valid. Where there is mutual gain and interest, a joint venture partnership may make sense if the opportunity is large and complex as the community development corporation may not have the resources to execute the work. Both partners must contribute valuable consideration for a partnership to be successful and sustainable. Aboriginal entrepreneurs can also provide valuable community benefits as they tend to hire a high percentage of community members.

The type of support you can provide an Aboriginal business includes:

- Improving health, safety, environment, and other management systems by providing meaningful feedback and in-kind resources to develop and implement management systems

- Marketing support on how to communicate with energy companies and contractors

- Providing information on standards and specifications

- Mentoring and coaching from senior management, technical, construction, operations, safety, and supply chain management

- Recommending potential joint venture business partners that are qualified, competitive, and preapproved by your business

- Providing feedback to Aboriginal business on how to improve their performance delivery and reinforce good performance on a regular basis in a more frequent manner than non-Aboriginal businesses

While this guidance is aimed at energy companies, much of the guidance is beneficial to contractors who sub-contract or desire to form partnerships with Aboriginal businesses.

Develop, nurture, and value these relationships for mutual gains. Develop and build your relationships with Aboriginal partners through active listening and discovery. You will discover that Aboriginal Businesses can contribute to problem solving and developing new opportunities. You will have to invest additional management and staff resources to develop Aboriginal business relationships but this can be time well spent, delivering benefits to both partners.

Tips for Successful Negotiations and Business Partnerships

When you work with Aboriginal people, you are doing business with another culture. Many benefits can result from these relationships, for both sides. Here are some tips to keep in mind to make negotiations and business partnerships more successful:

- **Take the initiative**—Do not wait for government to "solve" the issue of First Nations consent/cooperation. Take the time and make the effort to build an effective and trusting relationship. Relationships and contributing to improved community well-being will enable doors to be opened and continued economic growth.

- **Engage early and engage often**—It is never too early to start building relationships. And it takes a long time to get to an agreement – the worst thing to do is try to go too fast.

- **Treat each Nation individually**—First Nations are distinct, independent, and not all the same. Some Nations have fought wars against each other in the past. Today different Nations in BC may claim the same territory in treaty negotiations with government, so you may need to discuss your plan with more than one Nation. As a businessperson you cannot deal with Nation X in one way and then assume that the same approach will work with Nation Y. The Métis and Inuit each have a separate history and culture as well.

- **Think Asia**—In many countries in Asia, referrals from known and trusted contacts count, and face to face meetings are important. The same is true with many First Nations. It may take five or six meetings before you get down to business. Build the relationship first before you start discussing the details of what you want from the community.

- **The environment counts**—As a business seeking to work on First Nations traditional territory, you must address the importance of environmental issues as a first step towards reaching economic benefits. Communities look at the lands around them as their garden and water source. Industries are short term visitors while communities need the land and water for generations. Don't lead with dollars - lead with the environment.

- **History matters**—Whatever your business, remember that a long history of mistrust exists between Aboriginal and non-Aboriginal people in BC. Many are working hard to improve relations and are open to new approaches, but it's a work in progress. I've been party to meetings and presentations where tensions ran high and offense was easily taken. This is not to say that doing business is impossible, but rather highlights the importance of doing your homework and being prepared for all kinds of eventualities when you meet.

- **Work with the people who are there**—Different First Nations are at different stages of economic development, with some wealthier than others. Accordingly, their style of business dealings may be different from what you're used to. When in Rome, do as the Romans do.

One major interest of many Aboriginal leaders is to increase the capacity of their people. This goal can be challenging, as often Nations can afford only a small staff, some with limited business experience. More First Nations are studying commerce and economic development and are gaining business experience, so, with time, a community's capacity and capability will improve. In the meantime, some First Nations hire non-Aboriginal financial advisors, lawyers, communications consultants, and others to help them deal with government and resource project developers. Embrace these facts and work with the Nation and its advisors, not around them. Meeting only with the Chief may not be enough to advance your project or business activities.

- **Seek input and share decision making**—Ask for input and assistance in planning the work. Aboriginal people desire to have input and participate in decision making on activities that impact their livelihoods over multi-generations. Don't assume that you know what is best for a community or a business.

- **Keep in mind the broader needs**—As one advisor who works with First Nations said to me, "Many people ask me, 'What do First Nations want? They have all this new power but what do they want to do with it?' I believe each community is different and has unique needs, but many individuals want the same thing you and I or anyone else wants. A stable job, solid education for their kids, good healthcare, a clean and safe community, hope for the future. Right now some First Nation communities can lack some of these things. They are working to get there."

- **Have a sense of humour**—As Bob Joseph says, if you are working with a First Nation community, a sense of humour is definitely an asset. Visitors may be welcomed to a community with humour that sometimes bites a bit. Can you take some ribbing? Can you laugh at yourself, and can you handle it when others laugh at you? Go with the flow. Being teased with humour can actually be a sign of acceptance - a signal that people may want to work with you and are trying to include you and help you understand group norms.

Key legal considerations for developing joint venture partnerships with First Nations

By Roy Millen

When businesses look to form partnerships with First Nations, it is valuable to consider your legal needs and options. The first and most fundamental consideration is the underlying purpose of the arrangement.

There are a growing number of joint ventures (JVs) or partnerships between businesses and First Nations, typically seeking to work on other projects (private or public) in the First Nation's territory. In these arrangements, the business partner provides experience, expertise, and financial backing so that the JV can bid on contracts with commercial credibility. The aboriginal partner provides local legitimacy. Together, the JV can provide an attractive supplier for a project in the First Nation's territory that needs the particular capability provided by the business partner, but also wants to gain social licence.

Consider closely whether your proposed Aboriginal business partner can uphold its end of the bargain. Here are some of the questions: What is its governance structure? Are you dealing with an elected government or hereditary system, and which one has true authority to make the commitments you seek to secure from the First Nation? If the government is elected, when is the next election? Can you get an agreement executed before then? (Remember that these negotiations are rarely swift.)

What is the First Nation's territorial claim? Does it overlap with other First Nations' territories (which is likely), and if so, how much and where?

Consider your own capabilities, too. If you are promising to allocate a certain number of jobs to the First Nation's members, are you certain you will have the requisite number of positions available? Are a sufficient number of First Nation members available and interested? Are you prepared to train them? How long will that take?

Nothing ruins a relationship more swiftly than broken promises. With unemployment levels high in many aboriginal communities, members and their representatives will be very critical if promised jobs do not appear.

Last, consider how the terms of each agreement fit into your overall business and legal strategy. With JVs, consider whether you intend to form similar partnerships with neighbouring Nations and, if so, be aware of the potential for overlap disputes.

If you ask these questions early on and get answers before you make commitments, you will be able to establish your partnership on sound legal footing.

Roy Millen is a partner with Blake, Cassels & Graydon LLP. The above is excerpted from an article that first appeared in the April 28-May 4, 2015 edition of Business in Vancouver. Copyright Roy Millen. Used with permission.

Aboriginal Peoples as Employees

In Northern British Columbia, Aboriginal Peoples make up a considerable share of the population in several smaller urban areas. As shown in the table in Chapter 2, the Aboriginal population is significantly younger and growing faster than the province's general population, and so it is a labour supply you should consider in addressing your hiring needs.

The Aboriginal labour force is growing in size and level of education. High school graduation rates are increasing. In 2010/11 the numbers in apprenticeship training stood at 1,236; double that of 2006/2007. Many First Nations and Métis youth have developed successful careers in trades and technology. Aboriginal people are graduating from university in a variety of fields of interest to business. You may find some of your staff by contacting native student centres in universities and colleges throughout the province. Numerous young people and older adults move to larger urban areas to study, but would welcome a chance to return to their home communities with a good job waiting.

Gitwinksihlkw, Nisga'a Territory

Despite the advances in education, some Aboriginal people face barriers to participating in the wage economy. The most common include:

- Insufficient educational pre-requisites
- Lack of readiness at the community, family, and individual level
- Lack of access to transportation
- Lack of funding for trainees and training organizations
- Child and elder care responsibilities
- Employer willingness/capacity to sponsor apprentices
- Aboriginal awareness in employer organizations[8]

As an employer, you can play a positive role in the development of Aboriginal communities by hiring their people. Government financial assistance is available to individuals, training organizations, and employers and can significantly offset training costs and various programs can help remove barriers. In many cases, employers miss the opportunity to hire Aboriginal people because they lack awareness or knowledge on how to work with communities and their members. But by taking this step you will also benefit. If your workforce includes Aboriginal people, those individuals and their communities are likely to be more willing to support development if government and project proponents address some of their other concerns.

The benefits of hiring Aboriginal people go well beyond simply gaining access to their diverse skills. As an employer, you can expect to:

- **Gain a better understanding of concerns and interests of communities**. Aboriginal employees will enhance your ability to grow your business. They serve as your ambassadors with Aboriginal communities and improve understanding of how you manage your business activities. Good employment practices will create co-operative partnerships and collaborative community development.

- **Develop a stable and dedicated local workforce**. The turnover rate for Aboriginal employees at workplaces near Aboriginal communities is well below the national average.

- **Improve your decision making.** Diversity and inclusion in your workforce can be a key differentiator to achieving business success, competitiveness, and growth. When your employee base mirrors the demographics of nearby settlements, you will build stronger community relationships. An inclusive workplace environment that includes Aboriginal Peoples improves decision making and will demonstrate to all staff that your firm values different ideas, backgrounds, and perspectives.

27 Working Effectively with Aboriginal Peoples Must Do's ®

by Bob Joseph, President of Indigenous Corporate Training Inc.

1. Research your personal, your corporate, and your team's perspective on working with First Nation communities.

2. Take training on Aboriginal Awareness and Working Effectively with Aboriginal Peoples® before you start.

3. Research the community and governing parties before going to the community.

4. Plan activities by taking into account the timing of traditional practices such as fishing, hunting, and berry picking.

5. The Issue of Timing. Consider the issue of death in a First Nation community. Life is precious in any community, but population is a critical concern to communities struggling to grow as Nations. In this context it is not uncommon for all Band operations, including the Band office, to shut down completely following the death in a community. Try not to be disappointed if this happens to you.

6. Thank the community for the invitation into their traditional territory.

7. Use caution when shaking hands. The typical North American elbow grab and double pump may not be needed or appreciated.

8. Try to establish a relationship and meet before you need something.

9. Recognize that there are many dynamics at play when working with First Nation people and organizations.

10. Recognize that individual Nations like their autonomy (one First Nation cannot speak for another.)

11. Do everything possible to avoid sacred land issues by asking good questions and gaining understanding.

12. Learn about and stay up-to-date on Aboriginal issues and perspectives.

13. Consider dressing down for work in the community. In many cases, Band offices have more casual dress policies than does corporate Canada.

14. Be prepared to have your meetings recorded via microphone or video camera as some communities have had problems in their dealings with people who were less than honourable in remembering what they said.

15. Understand that internal community communications happen in many different ways.

16. Honour all your agreements, especially your oral agreements.

17. Approach issues with a joint problem-solving attitude.

18. Know the difference between a Band Chief and a Hereditary Chief before you visit an Aboriginal community.

19. Be prepared to possibly meet both Band Chiefs and Hereditary Chiefs on the same day and in the same meeting.

20. Try to match the conversation pattern of the people you are working with.

21. Be aware of who you are perceived to be aligned with when working in the community and manage those "people alignment" dynamics.

22. Aboriginal Peoples' rights are communally held.

23. Expect to participate in cultural events and ask for protocol guidance from the host.

24. Ask people "where they are from" to learn about where they likely stand on community issues.

25. Seek strategic placement for your organization's issues on community meeting agendas.

26. Be prepared to say that you are having a problem and that you are seeking their thoughts on how to solve it.

27. Anticipate questions they may have of your organization and prepare answers to those questions.

For full details and more information including an e-book: "23 what not to say or do's!" visit Bob Joseph's Indigenous Corporate Training Inc. website (www.ictinc.ca). There, you'll also find Bob's blog with close to 500 free articles on the subject of doing business with Aboriginal Peoples (www.ictinc.ca/blog/bc-first-nations) and a guide to terminology.

- **Contribute and support the community**. As a supplier of goods and services, you have an important role in providing economic benefits, which includes employment and training opportunities. Managing the impact of resource development is not only the responsibility of resource developers and government, but the contractor and supplier community as well.

Aboriginal Peoples as Customers

As noted previously, the incomes of Aboriginal people are increasing. The Aboriginal segment of the economy represents a rapidly growing consumer market and a potentially lucrative one for all Canadian businesses.

More specifically to British Columbia, in the Northeast, about 12 per cent of the population self-identified as Aboriginal. In Northwest BC, the figure is approximately one third of the population. In urban areas in the North, the largest concentration of Aboriginal people is in Prince Rupert (38.3 per cent of the total population), followed by Terrace (21.0 per cent).[9]

Throughout the North, First Nations living on reserves may have limited access to retail stores or the Internet for online shopping. So they will travel to larger centres to shop, obtain medical and other services, eat out, and enjoy local entertainment. Fort St. John in the Northeast, Prince George and Terrace and Prince Rupert in the Northwest are good examples of communities where businesses draw from a larger area that includes First Nations reserves, treaty lands, and traditional territories.

You can increase your presence with Aboriginal customers by sponsoring the many festivals and sporting and cultural events that take place in Northern BC. The CFNR Radio Network (First Nations Radio) is the only commercial content radio station broadcasting to over 50 First Nation communities and over 100,000 people in the Northwest, Central, and Northeast British Columbia. Some of the Aboriginal focused events CFNR attended in 2014 included the Annual All Native Basketball Tournament (Prince Rupert), Hobiyee 1st Nations Nisga'a New Year, Aboriginal Business Conference (Prince Rupert), and Haisla Days (Kitimat).

Another way to enhance your presence in the community is by simply attending social and cultural events with your staff and/or family or participating in fund-raising events. The Haisla, for example, organize a golf tournament in Vancouver each September to support children's activities in their home community in the Northwest. Or consider providing scholarships to local high schools or offering to send an employee to speak to students about careers in your industry.

Summary

As business partners, employees, or customers, if you do business in Northern British Columbia, you will likely engage with Aboriginal Peoples. This chapter has useful background information on Aboriginal business activities today and some candid and valuable advice from contributors with experience fostering cooperation and collaboration. Re-read the parts most relevant to your company, follow up on some of the suggested resources if you need to, and head to a conference or event of interest. Industry and Aboriginal communities in British Columbia are making real progress in forming meaningful partnerships; your business can be part of this success, too.

CHAPTER 4

A Dynamic Decade
Opportunities with the Major Projects

I'm fiercely Canadian. We live in a very wonderful country that allows people who don't have much to build something very quickly.

Alfred Sorensen, son of immigrants and CEO, Pieridae Energy Ltd.

This chapter explores in more detail the types of business opportunities available in Northern British Columbia. It first provides some background on the so-called major projects, ones worth billions of dollars, and then outlines some of the requirements for construction firms and others seeking to bid on them.

The Resource Industry in British Columbia's North

As the *Vancouver Sun* noted in a special report in September 2013:

A study in 2003 calculated that more than 70 per cent of B.C.'s export wealth is derived beyond the Lower Mainland and south Vancouver Island, a good proportion of it from the North. In the Northeast alone, the BC Business Council estimates industry investment in exploration and development of natural gas grew from $1.1 billion in 1999 to $7.9 billion in 2008. The natural gas sector employs 44,000 British Columbians directly and another 67,000 owe their jobs to it indirectly.

The North has 20 per cent of B.C.'s lumber mills, 35 per cent of its pulp mills and 27 per cent of its paper mills. It produces more than 30 per cent of the hydroelectricity, including almost 900 megawatts available from Alcan's Nechako reservoir. Mineral resources including molybdenum, gold, silver, copper and coal yielded more than 30 per cent of provincial mining revenues and in 2006 more than 70 per cent of mineral exploration in B.C., valued at $194 million, took place in the North.[1]

British Columbia's North is critical to the province's future growth and prosperity. An estimated $100 billion in industrial growth is proposed for the region with projects including mining, power, transportation, and potentially liquefied natural gas.[2]

Developing these projects will mean numerous contracts for construction companies and their suppliers. Given the remoteness of many of the proposed project locations, it also means work for environmental consultants, airlines, helicopters, camp service providers, food companies, and other service firms. Employment agencies, for example, need to recruit workers and train them in basic site orientation and safety. The list is endless.

As well, project proponents may spend millions, or even billions, before they make a final investment decision (FID), as they apply for environmental permits, explore, prepare sites, and so forth. Many of these firms will have requirements to provide opportunities for local contractors and for Aboriginal Peoples. Therein lies even more opportunity for firms that are located in the North.

In the decade ahead, all this activity, across multiple sectors, means that savvy, prepared companies working in Northern British Columbia can grow and prosper, as can the communities in which they're based. This chapter focuses on sectors with some of the largest proposed projects and lists examples of the business products and services they'll be procuring. These sectors include:

- Liquefied Natural Gas (LNG)
- Pipelines

- Refineries
- Site C dam and hydroelectricity project

Why the focus on projects in these sectors? If only a few go ahead, they will form a major element of the industrial backbone of the new North. The LNG industry is new to the North, but the province does have refineries, pipelines, and dams. The multi-billion dollar projects being proposed, however, are of a scale, complexity, and cost that is new to most working British Columbians. Proponents are still setting up their supply chains, which means new companies have a better chance at winning the contract. In contrast, bidding for contracts in the forestry, mining, and natural gas services sectors means trying to unseat long-established suppliers. So, the chapter also provides some tips and advice for small firms seeking to gain a foothold in major project construction.

Learning More

Premier's Natural Resource Forum, Prince George

(www.bcnaturalresourcesforum.com) – This Forum is held for three days every January in Prince George. It focuses on BC's natural resource industries and brings together senior resource sector, service and supply businesses, government, First Nations, and non-profit leaders. It's a great way to keep up on the latest in a variety of sectors.

Resource Works (www.resourceworks.com) – Non-profit organization focused on promoting dialogue on responsible resource development in British Columbia. Produces reports, articles, and other information for the public on key issues in the sector.

Business in Vancouver (www.biv.com) – Though focused on Vancouver, includes a monthly column on BC's North, and regular articles on northern industries and issues.

In addition, these large projects will generate spin-off effects with increased demands for retail, restaurants, hotels, and similar services in the communities near them. Logistics companies will thrive, as will maintenance contractors once sites are built. Again, the opportunities are abundant. See Chapter 1 for a listing of some of the sectors in communities that are poised to do well.

The Big Fish: Some Proposed Mega Projects

Below is some background information on some of the largest proposed projects in the North in the decade ahead.

Liquefied Natural Gas: New Industry, New Markets

As reported in the Globe and Mail:

> Alfred Sorensen had his "aha moment" in 2007 when he had a chance encounter with Randy Eresman, then chief executive officer of Encana Corp., at an investors symposium in London.

> Mr. Eresman asked what business he was in. Mr. Sorensen told him that he was leading a project to bring liquefied natural gas into British Columbia at Kitimat. The blunt reply from a man who was then heading one of Canada's largest oil and gas producers: "That's the stupidest idea I ever heard of."

> Mr. Sorensen went back to Calgary and told his partners they had a problem, that the nascent shale gas business throughout the U.S. and Canada was likely to flood the North American market. In a desperate effort to save their investment, they reversed course. Kitimat LNG became the first of what is now nearly 20 West Coast projects proposing to liquefy Canadian natural gas and export it to Asia.[3]

As discussed in Chapter 1, "The North Today," British Columbia has had a natural gas industry since the 1950s, with the primary export market being the United States. In 2013, pipelines transported 56 per cent of Canadian natural gas production to the US.[4] In 2000, with the introduction of new methods of releasing gas from shale, (known as hydraulic fracturing or "fracking" and horizontal drilling) this market started to dry up as the US increasingly sourced its own gas in the Bakken Fields of North Dakota and Montana. As a result, prices for natural gas in the United States have been dropping steadily since 2009. Producers in British Columbia have been forced to look for new customers in other countries.

With no end in sight for low prices, since 2010, companies have been developing proposals to build liquefied natural gas (LNG) plants on the Northwest coast, in Kitimat, Prince Rupert, and Stewart.

The diagram "Overview of Proposed LNG Production in BC" on the following page shows the basic steps to produce LNG industry in the province. The concept is to drill for gas in the Northeast, then, via new and existing pipelines, transport it to the Northwest Coast. In towns like Prince Rupert or Kitimat, companies would build LNG processing plants, which liquefy natural gas by cooling it. The companies then pump the gas into specialized tankers and ship it to offshore markets such as Japan and China.

Constructing these plants will enable British Columbia to diversify its exports and take advantage of the rapidly expanding Asian market. In British Columbia, the proposed LNG plants have captured headlines since early 2013. In the election of May 2013, the victorious BC Liberal Party made the development of a provincial LNG industry a central plank of its election platform. LNG development could inject as much as $9 billion a year into the province's economy.

To move ahead, proponents of LNG plant projects need:

- A secure source of gas from Northeast BC

- Access to a pipeline to transport the gas, with agreements from the First Nations along the route

- A plant site, with agreements with the First Nation(s) on whose territory it sits and provincial and federal environmental permits, agreements on taxes and royalties

- Specialized LNG carrier ships

- Large customers willing to sign 25-30 year agreements, typical in the sector

Between 2013 and 2015, governments and business were busy working to make the vision of a BC LNG industry a reality.

- Companies (also known as project proponents) applied for

Overview of Proposed LNG Production in BC

DRILLING IN NORTHEAST BC

(1) Drilling rigs drill vertical or horizontal wells to tap into natural gas reservoirs.

PROCESSING

(2) Processing plants separate natural gas from liquids and impurities. Liquids removed are used in other industries.

PIPELINES

(3) Natural gas is transported through pipelines from Northeast British Columbia to the Northwest Coast.

PROCESSING PLANTS IN NORTHWEST BC

(4) Processing plants cool the natural gas to -160°C and it becomes liquid.

DELIVERY TO GLOBAL MARKETS

 Specialized ships can then transport the liquefied natural gas (LNG) to global markets.

environmental and export permits with federal and provincial review agencies. In May 2014, seven joined together to form the BC LNG Alliance (bclnga.ca), pledging to collaborate in areas such as community outreach and labour training.

- In 2015, 19 different companies were exploring the possibility of constructing plants.

- Three major pipeline companies were conducting environmental assessments, planning routes, and consulting with First Nations. The provincial government negotiated a tax regime with the industry proponents and put in place revenue sharing agreements with First Nations. It also began spending millions more in educational institutions to train trades workers needed for LNG projects.

- First Nations negotiated benefit agreements with the companies proposing the projects.

- In February 2015, the Canadian government announced a major tax break for the industry, allowing companies to deduct 30 per cent of the cost of certain equipment purchases immediately—up from the previous eight per cent.

From a small business perspective, perhaps the most important activity was company spending related to LNG—even before any firm had made a final investment decision (FID). In May 2015, the Premier of British Columba, Christie Clark, estimated these expenditures to be in the order of $12.5 billion, on environmental studies, site preparation, impact assessment agreements with First Nations, and other goods and services.[5] Large companies are often prepared to spend $1-2 billion up front, as a way of reducing risks and costs should the project go ahead.

What's also important to realize is that no large player has actually made its final investment decision as of June 2015. Changing prices for natural gas, competition from other global sources (the United States and Australia, for example), the need to reduce construction and engineering costs, and finalizing agreements with Aboriginal Peoples will all play a role. Even if a company made an FID in 2015, a wave of other supplies globally means the first Canadian LNG exports from a large project will probably be pushed to the end of the decade or even 2023.

So, everyone was waiting. Still, even with the global downturn in oil prices as of 2014/2015, preparations continued, at the government, company, and community level. A small example: in May 2015, Simon Fraser University announced that it would be launching an Executive MBA program specifically tailored to Northwest British Columba. Classes will be taught in Prince Rupert and focus on key local industries: extractive resources, engineering, liquefied natural gas, and its related industries.

Optimists maintain that two or even three LNG plants might eventually be constructed in Northwest British Columbia, which means not only billions of investments in the plants, but also billions spent building pipeline infrastructure. Once the plants and pipelines are completed, companies will have to invest billions more on ongoing exploration and drilling in Northeast British Columbia, to keep those pipelines full. It's fairly easy to make the case that good business opportunities exist!

Tip

The Canadian Society for Unconventional Resources (www.csur.com) has excellent resource materials on unconventional hydrocarbon resources, focusing on: Shale Gas, Light Tight Oil, Gas Hydrates, Natural Gas from Coal, Tight Gas Sands and Carbonates. The Society provides and produces technical briefings and workshops and produce materials for a more general audience.

On the following pages are snapshots for companies interested in pursuing opportunities related to LNG. The first provides more details on LNG plant construction and the second, pipeline construction. Visit the websites listed for more current information, since these projects are ongoing.

Major Project Snapshot:
Construction of Liquefied Natural Gas Plants in Northwest British Columbia

The Projects

The building of large processing plants and export facilities to liquefy natural gas for export by ship to Asia. Plants, once completed, will employ 250-300 people. Construction normally takes five years and can involve up to 5,000 workers over the course of the project.

Status June 2015

Companies/consortiums had brought forward 19 possible projects. The largest plants were proposed for the towns of Kitimat and Prince Rupert on the Northwest Coast. No consortium had made a final investment decision, though Pacific Northwest LNG had made a conditional decision. They will have to weigh a complex mix of competitive factors-including outlooks for long term markets, tax and regulatory regimes, the general investment climate, labour costs, agreements with First Nations, environmental mitigation costs, and so forth.

Key Industry Associations and Supports

- **LNG Buy BC** (engage.gov.bc.ca/lnginbc)—A provincial government site listing business opportunities related to LNG projects. Register on the site to get regular updates.

- **Canadian Association of Petroleum Producers** (www.capp.ca)—Industry association with lots of background information on the natural gas sector.

- **BC LNG Alliance (bclnga.ca)**—Association of seven LNG proponents in British Columbia. The site has considerable educational material on the LNG sector.

Major Players

The table below provides details on the proposals for some of the largest LNG projects in Northern British Columbia, seen as having among the best chances of proceeding.

Project Name	Location	Companies	Pipeline to Transport Gas	Final Investment Decision Timing
Pacific NorthWest LNG (pacific-northwestlng.com) Investment for plant: $11 B	Prince Rupert	PETRONAS, Sinopec, JAPEX, Indian Oil Corporation, and Petroleum-BRUNEI	Prince Rupert Gas Trans-mission Line	Conditional approval, June 2015
LNG Canada (lngcanada.ca) Investment for plant: $12 B	Kitimat	Shell, KOGAS, Mitsubishi, and PetroChina	Coastal GasLink	Mid-2016 at the earliest
Kitimat LNG (www.chevron.ca/our-businesses/kitimat-lng) Investment for plan: $4.5 B	Kitimat	Chevron Canada and Woodside Energy International (Canada)	Pacific Trails Pipeline	Not stated but likely by end of decade

Types of Services Required – Construction Phase

LNG plants will require similar types of goods and services in many areas. Usually, a multinational Engineering, Procurement, Construction Management (EPCM) contractor will win the overall project to develop the site. (Companies like Bechtel and KBR have built LNG plants in Australia, for example, while Ledcor has done site preparation work for a proposed LNG facility in Kitimat). In turn, the EPCM contractor will release tenders suitable for local small and medium businesses later in the construction stage. Projects will need a broad range of suppliers, including:

- Civil and earthworks contractors
- Mechanical, electrical, instrumentation, and marine structure works contractors
- Heavy industrial fabricators
- Pre-engineered building design, fabrication, and assemblers
- Experienced LNG tank assemblers
- Experienced LNG tank concrete foundation and wall constructors
- Heavy industrial project freight forwarders
- Site support services
- Camp supply and support services

Advice from EPCM Companies

Multi-national Environment, Procurement, Construction, Management (EPCM) companies manage the overall construction of large facilities like LNG plants. Below is some of their advice to potential contractors.

- **Aboriginal partnering**—Certain construction-related services on projects may have been designated as Aboriginal opportunities, meaning businesses that are majority owned by Aboriginal people will get preference. In many cases, the Aboriginal entity will partner with other businesses that have long experience in these services.
- **Technical experience**—Contractors should have 3-5 years' experience. EPCMs may conduct quality checks on manufactured goods in the North. They have people there to inspect, and investigate sub-contractors to see if they can do the work before issuing the order.
- **Modern equipment**—As one interviewee said, "Don't try bringing your 1970s crane to our site. Everything should be up to code."
- **Insurance**—Ensure adequate insurance for commercial general liability, vehicle-related liability, and employer's liability. Many local suppliers have found they must increase their coverages.
- **Safety**—Many firms require safety documentation, WorkSafe BC Certificate of Recognition (COR), or for smaller firms, the Small Employer COR (SECOR) and a written drug and alcohol policy.
- **Registration**—Register with third party auditors like PCI for safety, Dun and Bradstreet for financial checks, and the EPCM's own database, so they can identify you as being interested in the specific project.

Major Project Snapshot:
Construction of Natural Gas/Pipelines in Northern British Columbia

The Projects

Construction of large (48 inch) pipelines to transport natural gas or petroleum. Natural gas would come from Montney natural gas play in Northeast British Columbia. Oil would come from the oil sands in Northern Alberta.

Status June 2015

Pipeline projects will proceed once an LNG plant or refinery proponent makes a final investment decision (FID).

Key Industry Associations and Supports

- **Canadian Energy Pipelines Association** (www.cepa.com)—The industry association of the major pipeline companies. Lots of general educational material.

- **BC LNG Alliance** (bclnga.ca)—Association of seven LNG proponents in British Columbia. Again, lots of educational material on the LNG sector.

- **Pipeline News North** (www.pipelinenewsnorth.ca)—Monthly newspaper with a focus on pipelines, LNG, and other energy issues in Northeastern British Columbia.

Major Players

The table on the following page provides details on the proposals for some of the largest proposed pipeline projects in Northern British Columbia.

Project Name	To-from Length	Company	Receiving LNG Plant or Oil Refinery	Final Investment Decision timing
Prince Rupert Gas Transmission Line (www.prince rupertgas.com) Investment: $5 B	Montney play (Hudson's Hope) to Prince Rupert 900 km	TransCanada	Pacific NorthWest LNG (pacificnorth westlng.com)	Late 2015
Coastal GasLink (www.coastalgas link.com) Investment: $4 B	Dawson Creek Area to Kitimat 650 km	TransCanada	LNG Canada (lngcanada.ca)	Mid-2016 at the earliest
Merrick Mainline Project (www.transcanada. com/merrick-mainline-project. html) connecting to Pacific Trails Pipeline (www.chevron.ca/ our-businesses/ kitimat-lng/pacific-trail-pipeline) Investment: Merrick-$1.9 B Pacific Trails - $1 B	Montney to Summit Lake, BC 260 km to Kitimat 480 km	TransCanada Chevron Canada and Woodside Energy International (Canada)	Kitimat LNG (www.chevron. ca/ our-businesses/ kitimat-lng)	Not stated but likely by end of decade
Eagle Spirit Pipeline Investment: Unknown	Alberta to Prince Rupert	Eagle Sprit Energy Holdings and Aquilini Group	Eagle spirit oil refinery	Unknown

Types of Services Required – Construction Phase

Contract Opportunities – Pre-Construction
- Right-of-way clearing
- Facility and storage area clearing
- Construction camp set-up
- Access road and bridge construction
- Support for pre-construction crews
  - Transportation
  - Catering
  - Vehicle and equipment supply and maintenance

Contract Opportunities – Construction Phase
- Vehicle and equipment supply and maintenance
- Pipe and vehicle hauling
- Gravel and fuel supply and trucking
- Hotshot delivery, crew transportation
- Access road construction and maintenance
- Concrete, rebar, fencing, hardware, lumber
- Hydrovac (locate cables, pipelines)
- Fire protection
- Environmental monitoring
- Administrative and clerical
- Right-of-way reclamation

Contract Opportunities – Operations Phase
- Facilities yard maintenance, right-of-way maintenance
- Equipment maintenance
- Water hauling and sewage removal
- Transportation and delivery services
- Airplane and helicopter rental
- Equipment rental
- Environmental monitoring

Figure 4: Proposed Major Pipeline Routes in Northern British Columbia

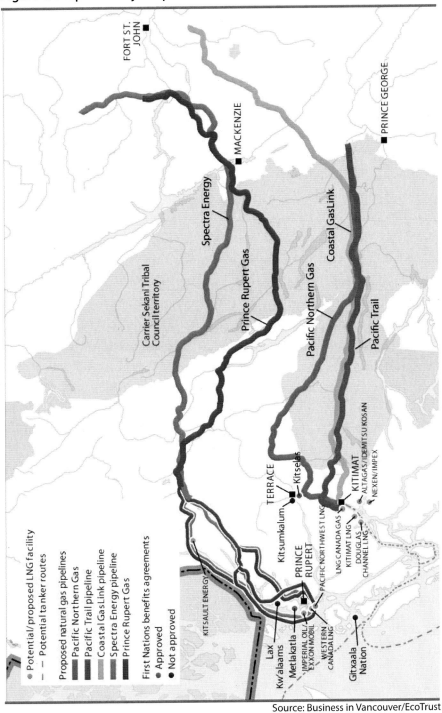

Site C: A major hydro-electric dam in Northeast British Columbia

Beginning in the 1960s, the government of British Columbia made major investments in large dams throughout the province. The resulting abundance of inexpensive electricity made BC an attractive place for investment.

After the mid-1980s, major dam building stopped, but the provincial population continued to grow. With an increase of 1.5 million people and proposals for liquefied natural gas plants (which consume enormous amounts of power) coming to the fore, in 2007, the government began reexamining a proposal to build a large new dam on the Peace River in Northeast BC, called Site C. Power from the facility would help meet future increases in demand for electricity.

Site C would be the third dam on the Peace River constructed since the 1960s. BC Hydro, the crown corporation the provincial government established in 1962 to manage electricity generation and distribution, had proposed building Site C in the 1980s and again in the 1990s. In April 2010, the provincial government announced that it would move forward with the project, which would be located about seven kilometers from Fort St. John.

Building Site C would take approximately eight years, with estimated costs in 2015 of almost $9 billion. At completion, the earth fill dam would be 60 meters high and 1,100 meters across, with a reservoir behind it covering 9,330 hectares. It would flood over 100 kilometers of a river valley.

The Site C project received environmental approvals from the federal and provincial governments in October 2014. In December 2014, the provincial government approved the project, with construction scheduled to start in the summer of 2015.

From the 2007 announcement onwards, the Site C proposal has faced strong opposition from Aboriginal Peoples, farmers in the area, scientists, and environmentalists. Their concerns include the effects of the large scale flooding of farmland, green house gas emissions, and the overall cost of the power generated, among others. Despite the opposition, BC Hydro has continued apace. It held meetings for potential suppliers, awarded contracts for site clearing and for managing the project camp (projected for 1,200 people), negotiated labour agreements, and so forth. Yet, with the announcement of lawsuits from First Nations in early 2015, it remains to be seen if significant construction delays will occur as these actions wind their way through the courts.

With a projected $9 billion in spending, ample opportunities exist for businesses, large and small. BC Hydro split the project into five phases. According to its website, in June 2015 it was at Stage 4, which would involve detailed engineering design work, project procurement, and early construction on roads, bridges, and diversion tunnels. The following Stage 5 would be construction, estimated to take about seven years.[6]

Proposed Site C dam when completed

Rendering provided courtesy of BC Hydro

Major Project Snapshot: Construction of Site C dam and hydroelectric facility

The Project

Construction of 1,100 metres wide, 60 metres high, earth filled dam on the Peace River, seven kilometers from the City of Fort St. John. Construction expected to last approximately seven years, to 2024, at an estimated cost of almost $9 billion. The facility will produce and supply about 5,100 gigawatt hours (GWh) of electricity each year to the province's integrated electricity system. For more information see www.sitecproject.com.

Status June 2015

Construction expected to start in the summer of 2015, but delays may occur because of lawsuits launched by First Nations in British Columbia and Alberta and a land owner group.

Major Players

BC Hydro (bchydro.com) is a provincial crown corporation. Its procurement approach consists of letting several large contracts for the major project components and multiple smaller contracts for supporting activities and ancillary works. Some of the major project components are listed below, with lead contractors identified where available.

Project Component	Lead Contractor	Contacts	Other details
Construction worker accommodations Camp will house 1,600 workers and others, for a total of 2,200 people.	Two Rivers Lodging Group	Pierre Landry, Territorial Sales Manager, ATCO Structures & Logistics Ltd. Email: tworivers@atcosl.com	

Environmental disposal Rather than disposal by burning or landfill dumping, BC Hydro has opted to try to find a greener solution to dealing with the organic materials site clearing produces.	Diacarbon Energy Inc.	www.diacarbon. com info@diacarbon. com	Diacarbon produces renewable fuels from biomass.
North Bank clearing Preparing the North Bank site of Site C dam construction will involve 7,000 meters of new access roads, excavating 3 million cubic meters of land; and clearing 115 hectares of land. 100 thousand cubic meters of aggregate material will be produced and stockpiled at the site.	None selected		RFP closed in March 2015. Contractor expected to be in place by early fall 2015.
Main civil works Approximately 32 million m³ of excavation for structures, including approach channel and tailrace. River diversion works, including construction of two 10.8 m internal diameter concrete-lined tunnels between 700 m to 800 m in length. Associated cofferdams and intake and outlet structures. Earth fill dam Roller-compacted concrete buttress Significant ancillary works such as permanent network of site roads, site drainage, and debris handling facilities	None selected		BC Hydro expects to select a contractor in fall 2015 or early 2016.

The Site C construction website provides a procurement forecast of upcoming opportunities and the status of current initiatives. Many other contracts will become available as the sub-station and transmission line are built in the years ahead. Keep current by visiting www.sitecproject.com.

Examples of Types of Services Required

BC Hydro's consultations showed that businesses in the region were interested in the following types of contracts.

Dam Site Components

- Archaeological site preparation
- Decommissioning of temporary access roads
- Environmental monitoring
- Offices, storage facilities, and staging areas
- Safety, first aid, and security
- Site re-vegetation
- Site road maintenance and snow clearing
- Transportation and shuttle services
- Truck washing and vehicle maintenance workshops
- Waste treatment and management facilities
- Workshops, labs, fabrication shops, and testing facilities

Off site components

- Accommodation support
- Boat launches
- Day use recreation areas
- Hudson's Hope shoreline protection
- Monitoring programs
- Operation of satellite worker accommodation camps (if required)
- Park and ride facilities
- Peace Canyon substation expansion construction activities
- RV site operation and management (if required)
- Wildlife or fish mitigation projects

Key Contacts

- **Site C Project Site** (www.sitecproject.com)—Check the business opportunities tab for updates on RFPs issued and contracts awarded. Register your firm with BC Hydro and identify the services you provide. Main Categories: Communications & Design, Construction & Engineering, Environmental Services, General Services, Hospitality.

- **BC Bid** (www.bcbid.gov.bc.ca)—Government procurement website where BC Hydro will put out major procurement projects for tender.

- **Lead Contractor websites**—Visit BC Hydro's site to identify the lead contractor for a project component. Then go to their website to register with the company or get more information.

Photo: PictureBC

City of Fort St. John

Refineries: Petroleum products made in British Columbia

If you've spent any time in British Columbia, you'll know that the transportation of bitumen via pipelines is a highly contentious topic. (Pipelines for natural gas are much less controversial, since if a rupture occurs, the gas largely dissipates into the air.) The diluted bitumen or heavy oil to be moved comes from the oil sands of Alberta, the province adjacent to BC. Even more opposition faces proposals to then transport the bitumen in ships to overseas markets. Aboriginal Peoples and environmentalists maintain that pristine marine environments could be fouled for decades if a major spill occurs; they point to the impact of the Exxon Valdez spill in Alaska in 1989, with negative effects on beaches and wildlife still present 25 years later. [7]

Since 2012, attempts by Enbridge, a major pipeline company, to build the Northern Gateway pipeline for transporting Alberta heavy oil to the BC coast have met with fierce, ongoing resistance. (As I travelled throughout the Northwest in 2012, I saw signs, on Haida Gwaii and throughout the mainland, marked, "Say No to Enbridge!") Some now wonder if the pipeline will ever be built.

One company's problem is another's opportunity. As Alberta continued to seek overseas customers for its petroleum products, and BC for its natural gas, four refinery and upgrader proposals had emerged by 2015. All offered alternatives to shipping raw products by sea.

Refineries for heavy oil would be new to the Canadian scene. The country has facilities to handle light crude and also upgraders that transform heavy crude to lighter crude. Most heavy oil refining, however, is carried out in the United States. As well, refining is typically carried out close to the market that consumes the product, rather than close to the resource.

As of 2015, three proposed bitumen refineries and their locations included:

- Pacific Future Energy (Prince Rupert or possibly elsewhere)
- Kitimat Clean (Kitimat)
- Eagle Spirit Energy (Northeastern BC or Northern Alberta)

A fourth proposed project has been put forward by Blue Fuel Energy. Their plant would make methanol from natural gas, which would then be transformed into a low-carbon gasoline, using the hydrogen and oxygen parsed from water. The fuel and methanol the plant produced would be shipped by rail. The process is not unheard of: in the 1980s and 1990s, a plant in New Zealand produced about 14,000 barrels per day of unleaded gasoline from natural gas based methanol. The scale of the plant in British Columbia, however, would be much larger.

All these plants face technical challenges of one sort or another and, as with proposed LNG plants, project proponents will need to be innovative and creative—and have deep pockets. Estimated construction costs range from $3-30 billion.

No construction has started on any of the plants, but two, Eagle Spirit Energy and Blue Fuel Energy, say that they have strong First Nations support. Blue Fuel Energy may make a final investment decision by the end of 2015. Other proponents are carrying out feasibility studies, assessments, and so forth.

Tip: Learn jargon digitally!

Check out the Handyman Glossary, an I-phone application that provides a glossary of commonly used industry terminology, lingo, descriptions, equipment, and definitions. Available at www.macworld.com.

On the following pages is a snapshot for companies interested in pursuing opportunities related to refineries. Visit the websites listed for more current information, since these projects are ongoing.

Major Project Snapshot:
Refineries in Northwest and Northeast BC

The Projects

The building of large refineries to process heavy oil or natural gas to refined products such as gasoline, diesel, and jet fuel to transport by rail or ship to customers. Construction normally takes five years or more and can involve up to 5,000 to 10,000 workers over the course of the project.

Status June 2015

Companies/consortiums had brought forward four possible projects. Refineries were proposed for the towns of Kitimat and Prince Rupert on the Northwest Coast, Chetwynd in the Northeast and another possible location in the Northeast. No major consortium had made a final investment decision. They will have to weigh a complex mix of competitive factors—including outlooks for long term markets, tax and regulatory regimes, the general investment climate, labour costs, agreements with First Nations, environmental mitigation costs, and so forth.

Key Industry Associations and Supports

- **Canadian Association of Petroleum Producers** (www.capp.ca)—Industry association with lots of background information.

- **Company/Consortium websites**—Visit the proponent's site (listed on the following page) for up-to-date information. In 2015, these projects were still in the early stages.

- **Pipeline News North** (www.pipelinenewsnorth.ca)—Monthly newspaper with a focus on pipelines, LNG, and other energy projects in Northeastern British Columbia.

Major Players

The table below provides details on the proposals for refinery projects proposed for Northern British Columbia.

Project Name	Location	Transportation of refined product	Details
Pacific Future Energy (www.pacificfutureenergy.com) Refinery investment: $10 B	3 options in general Prince Rupert area	Rail, possibly pipeline in future	Would eventually have 5 modules, total investment of $30 B
Kitimat Clean (kitimatclean.ca) Refinery investment: $21 B Pipeline and shipping fleet: $11 B	Kitimat	Pipeline from Edmonton and then via tanker fleet	Would be engineered to be the cleanest upgrading and refining site in the world
Eagle Spirit Energy (No specific website available) Refinery investment: $30 B Pipeline: $15-20 B	Northeast	Refinery in Northeast BC or Alberta, port for tankers in Prince Rupert or other port, but not Kitimat	Company partners include leading Aboriginal business leaders and Aquilini Development and Construction Inc., of Vancouver
Blue Fuel Energy (bluefuelenergy.com) Refinery investment: $3.8 B	Chetwynd	Rail	Final Investment Decision expected late 2015

Types of Services Required—Construction Phase

As of June 2015, companies proposing pipelines were still seeking to raise capital, obtain agreements with First Nations, and complete feasibility studies. Construction of projects will be some years away and will likely involve many of the site preparation activities that the other large plants/facilities require.

Suppliers to Major Projects: Welcome to the Big Leagues

As outlined earlier, companies are planning billions of dollars in investment in the North. Even if only a small number of projects go ahead, numerous business opportunities will still be available in construction and operations of the natural gas and liquefied natural gas, mining, and alternative energy sectors, as well as the indirect and induced demand for other services.

Photo: Initiatives Prince George

Much of the work up to 2020 and beyond will be construction related. The multinational owners of these projects often prefer to hire as many qualified local workers as possible; it's more cost effective as it reduces the size of camps and the number of workers who fly in and out. In many cases, these project proponents will encourage their contractors to partner or subcontract with Aboriginal businesses, since they have negotiated agreements to engage First Nations businesses and employees. In addition, the project proponents want to contract with local companies that can complete the work at a competitive cost and perform it in a safe manner. For project proponents, a basic challenge is just to identify firms in the North that can meet their business needs, including the safety and procurement requirements. In July 2014, Northern Development Initiative Trust estimated that only 20 per cent of local businesses had websites.[8]

Many northern firms have little or no experience working on projects worth billions of dollars and are frequently unprepared for the stringent requirements of project proponents. Informal business processes are generally unsuited to complex projects guided by multinationals that have a disciplined approach to contracting and procurement activities. As one small business owner said to me in Terrace, "You can't just show up on site in an old truck and expect to start working." Instead, formal contracting and procurement processes, safety and other management system requirements, and so forth, are the order of the day.

If the major projects are a target market, how do you position your company to obtain contracts? Besides having a website so project proponents can find you, (see Chapter Six, "A Business Road Map" for ideas on setting one up), the following pages lay out some other basics you need to have in place.

Health, safety, and environmental management systems: A Non-negotiable requirement

For quite a few small enterprises, implementing a health and safety management system acceptable to project proponents and their contractors can be a real challenge. Many lack the staff and knowledge to set up a system unique to their company (just copying someone else's may not do the trick!), and the time to send staff to appropriate courses and do the required follow up.[9]

But for project proponents, ensuring a safe workplace is their first priority, and they will only work with contractors and suppliers who can meet their requirements. They want companies working on their sites to have formal health, safety, and environment programs that enable the identification and control of hazards associated with the work. They require contractors to submit their plans for approval and have a third party audit them.

Safety Makes Good Dollars and Sense

Your operation is small with only three employees. They are solid workers, careful. You've never had a serious accident or fatality. You don't need an occupational health, safety, and environment (HSE) Program—right? You might be a sole proprietor or owner operator. You don't need to think about health and safety, let alone implement a HSE Program. Let's take a moment to think that through.

You are called out to a remote job site and you attend the site alone. What is your "report in" or "working alone" protocol? Who knows where you are going? Your expected return time? The route you are driving? Having in place a basic "report in" or "working alone" protocol, even as a sole proprietor/owner operator might be the difference between life and death. In British Columbia, the *Workers Compensation Act (the "Act")* and the Occupational Health and Safety Regulations, Part 3, requires an employer to initiate and maintain a (formal) occupational health and safety program when they have a workforce of 20 or more workers **and** at least one workplace that is determined to create a moderate or high risk of injury **or** if you have a workforce of 50 or more employees. This does not, however, mean smaller operations are exempt. If the workforce is less that the number outlined above, the employer **must** initiate and maintain a less formal program.

The legal requirement as described above is prescriptive (you "must"). I want to point out the difference between implementing a health and safety program because of a legal requirement and creating and implementing a health and safety program because it makes smart business sense in the short and long term. Building your business from the ground up with a health and safety focus is good business.

Most large companies use a broker firm to screen potential contractors. These organizations collect and verify contractor health and safety data.

12 Tips for Creating an Occupational HSE Program

1. Conduct a work/risk assessment of your operation based on the number of employees, sites, job tasks, and risk, etc.

2. Do a gap analysis through a neutral third party. Are you seen as an employer who sends mixed messages about safety versus productivity? A good program also includes regular periodic reviews/audits.

3. Based on a comprehensive understanding of risk and gaps, build an Occupational Health, Safety, and Environment program that meets your company needs and service offering.

4. Consider using systematic approaches to HSE: for example, hazards

and effects management processes (identify, assess, control, recover) and use a plan/do/check/improve approach. Use tools such as a hazard register, hazard identification (hazid) checklists that include health, safety, security, and environmental hazards and job safety analyses.

5. Involve your employees in building and implementing the program. Commitment to the program from the grass roots to the leadership is imperative. Safety is everyone's responsibility.

6. Accountability is key. Where does the health and safety portfolio reside? Who is responsible for what? What about the reporting structure?

7. Record, record, record. Investigate, investigate, investigate. Record every injury or potential injury: a cut, a sprain, a near miss, etc. Investigate every incident. What happened? What could we do differently? Review records weekly since they provide information about what might need to be done differently.

8. Conduct weekly, unscheduled inspections to see how work is being done on site.

9. Build regular safety meetings into your team's schedule. Once you have compiled the data from the records, look for trends and talk about the trends and provide training as needed. Create a paper trail demonstrating due diligence.

10. Be proactive. Safety includes both personal and process safety. Consider developing a management of change (MOC) process.

11. Prior to starting each new job, think about health, safety, and the environment. What are the hazards? What kind of equipment is required? What training is needed?

12. Train each new employee in the health, safety, and environmental requirements/protocols of your company. Be clear about the expectations and consequences. Have the employee and the administrator sign off on the orientation.

Cherie Williams, President of The Parallax Perspective, has over 25 years' experience in workers compensation. She and her team work primarily with small and mid-sized businesses designing and developing health, safety, and environment programs, claims management systems, and return to work programs tailored specifically to company needs in concert with the training required to both implement and sustain these programs. As a workers compensation expert, she writes employer submissions and represents employers in the review and appeal process. She can be reached at cheriewilliams1@me.com.

Prequalification Systems: Sign up or sign out

Most project proponents require contractors to have their HSE management systems and performance verified by third party audit service providers. Essentially, these companies provide web-based data management systems for project proponents and general contractors. They don't conduct audits of your work site(s), but instead perform a desk top review and verification of documents, data, and certifications that your firm sends to them. The prequalification and verification requirements for health, safety, and environmental systems vary by industry. Some third party audit service providers that project proponents in British Columbia use include:

- *ISNetworld* – www.isnetworld.com
- *ComplyWorks* – www.complyworks.com
- *PICS* – www.picsauditing.com

If you're planning to bid on a project, identify the third party audit service provider that the project proponent uses. One project may use PICs, another ISNetworld. Call their procurement department to find out. When bidding on multiple contracts with different proponents, you may have to subscribe to more than one of these services. The costs in time and money can quickly add up, so it's best to be thoughtful about the number you subscribe to and maintain the data as current.

Human Resources (HR) Systems

For many small and even larger firms, human resources is viewed as a cost area, and sometimes offers little beyond handling the payroll, attendance management, and benefits. (I've visited 250 person firms where the "HR person" was the Executive Assistant to the President and looked after HR on a part time basis.)

To be taken seriously in the world of major projects, your company will need to have a basic HR system in place. At a minimum, it should have:

- **Current, written job descriptions**—Some companies have either no job descriptions, vague paragraphs, or descriptions someone put together 10 years previously. In a tight labour market, you need to know who you want to hire and the skills and the experience they

BIDDING ON PROJECTS: SOME BASICS

RESPONDING

- Companies issue different types of requests—Expressions of Interest, Pre-qualifications, Requests for Proposal.
- Register with the issuer, if required.
- Read the document carefully—what are the requirements, exceptions, change orders, audit requirements, payment terms, and evaluation criteria?
- Don't meet the mandatory requirements? Move on. Only promise what you can deliver.
- Ask questions if needed.

IF YOU WIN

- You're signing a binding legal contract. Have your lawyer look at it.
- Prepare for audits—field verification, performance audit, site monitoring.
- Secure financing if needed—payment terms may be 120 days or longer. There may be holdbacks.

IF YOU LOSE

- Ask for a debriefing—find out ways to improve your bid for future opportunities. Be persistent to get guidance more meaningful than, "you're not competitive."
- Asking smart questions makes your company look professional—and there are always other opportunities.

need and communicate that message clearly. If you have no idea how to develop a good job description, look online at O*NET- (www. doleta.gov/programs/onet/eta_default.cfm), a great resource that the American government has developed. As the website notes, "The O*NET database is a comprehensive source of descriptors...for more than 900 occupations. This includes: skills, abilities, knowledge, tasks, work activities, work context, experience levels required, job interests, work values/needs, and work styles." The Appendices include a sample job description for a construction worker, along with sample interview questions.

- **Competitive compensation**—As mentioned in the previous section, if you're offering pay and benefits below market rates, you'll have a tough time attracting good candidates.

- **Training**—Many small business owners have said to me, "I don't like to pay for training since the person either leaves or gets poached (hired away) by another firm." Poaching happens, it's true, but if you provide no training, it's even more likely the person will leave. You also need to keep good records of training for insurance and liability purposes.

- **Good processes for managing employees**—The HR term is "performance management." You need to have even a simple process in place for:
  - Linking individual employee objectives with your strategic plans and business objectives. Staff need to understand how they're contributing to the achievement of the overall business goals.
  - Setting clear performance objectives and expectations. People need to know what they're supposed to do and how you expect them to do it.
  - Developing training and development plans for each employee.
  - Providing coaching, mentoring, feedback, and assessment as needed.

Summary

The major projects in the North are constantly changing, so visit the websites listed to get the most current information. If you're prepared and ready to work hard, they offer major opportunities to businesses large and small.

PART 2

Staking Your Claim

Near Dawson Creek, British Columbia

CHAPTER 5

Travelling and Living in the North

A ship in port is safe, but that's not what ships are built for.

Admiral Grace Hopper

To set up a business in Northern British Columbia, you'll need to take a trip to the region. You might eventually decide to settle in one of its communities. This chapter is about some fundamentals of travelling and living in the North.

Watching the Weather

Northern British Columbia is large enough to contain the countries of France and Germany. It stretches from the temperate rainforests of Haida Gwaii on the west coast to the boreal forests of Fort Nelson in the North. It is a land of varying and often extreme weather, the effects of which can be magnified by the limited infrastructure in some places. Working within the dictates of climate and location is not only sensible, but essential.

Tip: Time Your Trip For Success

Where possible, plan your trip during the warmer months. Flying tends to be better from April to October. If you're planning to drive, April through November is generally fine in the Northwest and North Central, mid-May to early October in the Northeast.

Airline Travel

Flying is a convenient way of covering the distances in Northern BC, especially in the snowy months of winter. Some airports are increasingly busy; in 2014, Northwest Regional Airport (Terrace/Kitimat) logged a record 253,368 passengers. Airports are smaller, but with the surge of activity in the North, most are modern and many are in the process of expanding and improving their facilities. Fort Nelson received $4.3 million in 2014 to upgrade its runway. In 2014-2015, Prince Rupert is spending $20 million to improve its runway and terminal building. Fort St. John airport has allocated almost $5 million to upgrade its parking, water, and sewer facilities. Prince George has a larger airport, with regular flights to Vancouver and Calgary.

Airlines serving Northern BC include Air Canada, Westjet, Hawkair, Central Mountain Air, and Pacific Coastal Airlines. Charters from Northern Thunderbird Air and Guardian Aerospace are also available. On weekdays, flights from Vancouver are frequent, especially to Prince George, Kitimat/Terrace, and Fort St. John. In 2015, Air Canada and Westjet added direct flights from Calgary to Terrace.

With the advent of Westjet flights from Vancouver to Fort St. John and Terrace in 2013, ticket prices have become much more competitive. These routes are extremely busy so it's best to book well ahead both for availability and a good fare.

Table 5.1 on the following page shows the number of flights on weekdays from Vancouver during the winter of 2015. Flights are available on weekends, albeit less frequently. Many Northerners I've spoken to will plan a quick weekend getaway to Vancouver to catch a hockey game or concert or do some shopping—flights from most communities are under two hours.

Airline security can be strict; I've had items confiscated in Northern airports that sailed through screening in Vancouver. (On the other hand, Fort Nelson airport has no security checkpoint. You have to land in Dawson Creek or Fort St. John to do the security screening, before moving on to Vancouver or other places.) When you make your trip, you may encounter small planes, some older, with tight seating and limited room for luggage in overhead bins. (Some flights offer a "sky check" service, allowing you to leave your hand luggage on a cart before you enter the plane.) Be prepared for crowded planes. Most of my flights to and from smaller locations have been filled with well-built tradesmen heading back to or home from work camp, older people or young mothers returning from medical appointments, and sun-seeking Northerners on holidays, especially in the winter. It can get a bit bouncy at times, too, as the smaller, propeller-driven planes push through storms and/or battle high winds off the ocean. (On occasion, landings on Haida Gwaii can demand a particularly strong stomach.)

Table 5.1: Flights from Vancouver to Northern Communities, Winter 2015 Weekday Schedule

Vancouver to:	Prince Rupert	Terrace/ Kitimat	Smithers	Prince George
Total Daily Flights	3	11	3	10
Airlines Serving Town/Number of daily flights				
Air Canada	2	5	2	5
Central Mountain Air		2		
Hawkair	1	2	1	
West Jet		2		5

Vancouver to:	Fort St. John	Fort Nelson	Dawson Creek
Total Daily Flights	6	1	1
Airlines Serving Town/Number of daily flights			
Air Canada	4		
Central Mountain Air		1	1
Westjet	2		

Weather and mechanical delays can be other factors to keep in mind. Prince Rupert is notorious for its foggy mornings in winter, leading to frequent flight delays. Snowstorms can take their toll; in February 2015, Terrace/Kitimat airport closed as the region dealt with two metres of snow that fell in four days! As well, some older planes can be subject to issues. A colleague travelling from Calgary to Fort St. John started on one plane, switched to another because of mechanical issues, and then it had to turn back, again for technical problems, and finally landed in Fort St. John 10 hours later. (Normally, the flight takes slightly under two hours.) She then boarded her return flight back to Calgary, which left 30 minutes after she arrived!

Trains, Buses, and Ferries

Via Rail Canada offers passenger rail service on its Skeena route from Prince Rupert to Prince George, twice a week in winter and three times a week in the summer months. It's largely a tourist train, and as freight trains on the tracks have the right of way, frequent delays occur. The scenery, though, is gorgeous and offers views that rival those in the Canadian Rockies.

Bus service is available through Greyhound to most of the major towns in the North. Generally, the service is best for backpackers and travellers with a lot of time.

To reach Haida Gwaii, you can take a BC Ferry from Prince Rupert, which takes about seven hours. In winter, the waters can be quite rough, so you may want to fly if you're prone to sea sickness.

Traveller's Tip: Making the Call

Cell phone coverage can vary throughout the North. Ask the locals about dead spots before you head out on a road trip, both for safety reasons or if you're expecting an important call. If it's important you stay in touch at all times, consider renting a satellite phone.

Major Regional Highways

The major highways in Northern British Columbia include:
- Highway 97 via 1 or 99, links Vancouver to Prince George
- Highway 16 links Prince George to Prince Rupert while passing through such communities as Smithers, Terrace, and many others along the way
- Highway 37 (Stewart-Cassiar Highway) links Kitimat to Terrace, merges with Highway 16, then heads north at Kitwanga to the Yukon border
- Highway 97 links Prince George to Fort Nelson. Dawson Creek and Fort St. John are other larger communities on the route
- The Alaska Highway is part of Highway 97, which begins at Mile Zero in Dawson Creek and continues to Watson Lake, Yukon

Figure 5: Highways in Northern British Columbia

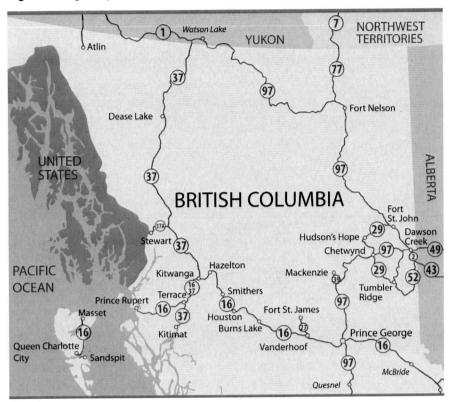

Roads in the region are generally well maintained, though delays can occur if crews are repairing a piece of key infrastructure. This maintenance often causes delays of 30-40 minutes as the site can stretch for several kilometers and have extremely dusty conditions. Often a pilot vehicle guides the traffic through the construction zones. As an example, in September 2011, severe rainfall washed out a large section of Highway 37, leading north from the lodge at Bell II to Dease Lake. Cars had to travel through the section in a convoy, following a pilot car, taking turns heading north or south. In September 2012, a large truck knocked out portions of the bridge at Bell II and traffic was reduced to a single lane, only open at set times. In both years, if you missed your turn, you waited for three hours or more for the next opportunity to continue your journey. By coincidence, I was caught up by these problems both years on my way up to visit the Tahltan First Nation.

Highway driving in the winter can be dangerous. Parts of northern routes are quite remote and if you encounter problems it may be hours before help arrives. Wise travelers carry a sleeping bag in their vehicle in case they are stranded, since temperatures can dip to minus 40° Celsius. Even the locals are cautious and know that roads can close frequently due to weather conditions. Unless you're accustomed to travelling on isolated routes with potentially severe winter driving conditions, it's best to fly or plan your visit for another time. Another concern is wildlife. It's abundant in the North and drivers need to always be on the lookout, since a collision with a moose can be fatal.

Pilot Car, Highway 37

Car Rentals

Car rentals are available throughout the North. Some towns like Fort Nelson have only one service provider; larger centres may have two or three. For the best deals, it's sometimes best to contact the local franchise office. I've saved quite a few dollars by calling them directly to book, rather than relying on the central office/online sites.

Always reserve well ahead of time. Although they're constantly expanding their fleets, rental agencies can run short of vehicles. Once, I arrived in

Fort St. John on a Tuesday in January with a colleague, who had assumed we could arrange for a vehicle upon arrival. Not so, as all three agencies were fully booked. With no taxis in sight we were fortunately able to hitch a ride to our meeting with a pair of friendly BC Hydro trainers, who knew the drill and had reserved in advance.

Finally, in some towns and on certain stretches of highway, gas stations can be limited and may close earlier than you're used to. Know their location and hours of operation to avoid expensive charges for returning a vehicle without a full tank. When you're out on the road, you also need to plan your trip carefully and time your fill-ups. As an example, on the highway between Watson Lake and Fort Nelson, even in summer months no gas stations are open after 10:00 pm. One traveler I spoke to mentioned he had run out of gas at 3:00 a.m. 18 kilometres outside of Fort Nelson on that stretch of highway. The terrain is hilly and he used more gas than expected.

Traveller's Tip: Ask About the Tires

If you're planning to drive outside the town in winter, ask in advance about the tires on your rental vehicle. You want snow tires and they are not standard issue – you have to request them. Preferably the vehicle will also have chains available. Trucks or SUVs with four wheel drive are usually better than cars for travelling on winter roads.

Taxis/Shuttles

Taxi service is generally available in larger northern communities with airports, although you may face waits. In bustling places like Fort St. John, all the hotels recommend pre-booking. You may get lucky and have a taxi appear at the airport, but don't be surprised if other travellers ask if they can pile in with you. People grab a cab when they can! Smaller towns like Vanderhoof and Fraser Lake have no taxis; so it's smart to ask ahead if service is available in a community you're visiting.

Some of the larger hotels offer shuttles, as does the Prince Rupert airport. The airport is on an island and provides bus service for passengers to a ferry that then takes you to the mainland.

Accommodation

Accommodation, like the weather, varies greatly across Northern BC. Entrepreneurs are scrambling to erect new hotels in under-served towns like Kitimat and Terrace. In Prince George, major hotels like the Coast are sprucing up their properties to compete with newer offerings like the Sandman. In the Northeast, numerous hotels and motels have sprung up over the past 10 years and more are being built.

Particularly in the Northeast, prices can be stiff, especially in the summer when tourists compete for sometimes limited space.

As with rental cars, it's wise to book your lodgings well in advance. All year round, good hotels can be completely filled with company employees working nearby or travelling through. If you leave your booking to the last minute, a good chance exists you won't find any availability or will have to pay a premium or travel to the next town. I was caught in Terrace one night when the last flight was unable to leave due to fog in Vancouver. Fortunately my friendly bed and breakfast hosts were able to put me up at the last minute. Many less fortunate travelers spent the night on the airport floor, since no rooms were available at local hotels.

Room rates generally include a full breakfast, with meat, eggs, fruits, cereals, breads, and pastries. Breakfast is typically available starting at 5:00 or 5:30 a.m. until 9:00 a.m. or so on weekdays.

Based on my years of business travel throughout Northern BC, my advice is to look for quality accommodation and be ready to pay accordingly. If you're unfamiliar with the community, ask your local contact for suggestions or take a browse through an online rating site like Trip Advisor. In the North, when it comes to hotels and motels, you truly get what you pay for. Trying to save a few dollars on a stay may leave you sleepless, grumpy, and unprepared for important meetings.

The other option to consider, particularly if you're on your own, is a bed and breakfast. While limited in the Northeast, Prince George, Smithers, and the Northwest coastal towns boast some lovely places. Most offer Internet connections and other business necessities, full breakfasts, and a friendly local to offer directions and tips. Some even have suites with kitchens to rent; ideal if you're staying in an area for a while and want to eat more than restaurant fare each night.

Traveller's Tip: Some Great Bed and Breakfasts

I'm often on my own when travelling in the North, so I welcome a chance to kick back and relax in the more homey atmosphere of a bed and breakfast. Below are two of my favourites:

Terrace—My favorite place to stay in the North is "Remo Ridge Bed and Breakfast" located outside of Terrace, on the way to the airport. Hosts Mark and Colleen Annibal are warm and welcoming and the rooms are immaculate. They also rent out a downstairs suite with two bedrooms, a living room, and full kitchen. Phone: 250-638-0989, Email: markcolleen@telus.net.

Prince George—Water's Edge Bed and Breakfast is a lovely, spacious home right along the river. Stuart and Marie Willmot are marvellous hosts and the views are spectacular. Toll Free: 888-567-3311, Email: wilmostuart@yahoo.ca.

(Note that I make these recommendations independently and received no reimbursement of any sort from the owners.)

Cuisine—Take Out, Cooking, or Restaurants?

Other than in Prince George, dining out options in Northern BC seldom go beyond well-known chains. In the North, franchises like Boston Pizza and Brown's have some of the highest sales in all of Canada. Prince Rupert is known for its seafood restaurants, and throughout the region larger hotels often offer decent fare. Part of the challenge in busy towns is keeping staff; better paying opportunities are often readily available in the local resource industry. As a result, in some communities you may deal with limited dining options, with skeleton staff and slow service.

In some communities, it may be faster (and healthier) to cook your own meals or buy take out. Many hotels and motels offer microwaves and fridges. Northern communities will generally have large grocery chain stores like Safeway, IGA, or Save-On-Foods, that offer a variety of take-out, hot food, salads, and so forth. Prices are reasonable and the quality is surprisingly good, considering the remoteness of many towns.

Living in the North

Eventually you may decide to relocate your business to the North and live there full time. Below are some fast facts to prepare you for what to expect.

Housing

Buying a Home

For many people from the Vancouver area of British Columbia (where average housing costs are second highest in the world, after Hong Kong), the low cost of housing is one of the major attractions of living in the North. It's not dirt cheap everywhere; some towns like Fort St. John have housing prices comparable to Chilliwack or Langley, suburbs of Vancouver. Still, many young people are moving North because of the more affordable housing and higher incomes. As noted in an article in *Business in Vancouver* in February 2015[1]:

> In May, Heidi De Wildt, 26, and her 27-year-old husband, Richard, decamped from Metro Vancouver, selling their townhome and moving to Prince Rupert on British Columbia's northwest coast. The De Wildts sold their Port Coquitlam townhouse for $368,000. They immediately bought a two-storey, four-bedroom house in Prince Rupert for $325,000 – and both have landed jobs in the community.
>
> Scott McWalter, 29, and his fiancée, Crystal Paten, 30, bought a five-year-old, four-bedroom detached house in an upscale Prince George neighbourhood after moving from Vancouver. The $400,000 house they settled on is the type of two-storey, mid-level executive that would cost at least $1.3 million in Vancouver.

This pattern of good homes at decent prices is a constant across the region. The table on the following page shows the average housing prices in the major communities.

Rental Costs

Many new Northern homebuyers buy houses with a rental suite to generate extra income. It's a smart strategy in a region with some of the lowest vacancy rates and highest rents in the province. In Dawson Creek and Fort St. John, an average two-bedroom apartment rents for around $1,100, according to Canada Mortgage and Housing Corporation's 2015 spring survey, second only to Vancouver. In Terrace, Prince Rupert, and Kitimat in the Northwest, vacancy rates are below one per cent.

As can be seen in Table 5.2, rental costs in the region differ, but if the community is undergoing an economic boom, prices tend to reflect it. (If you're in residential housing construction, a business opportunity obviously exists!)

Table 5.2: Housing and Rental Costs in Selected Northern Communities

Location	Average House Price 2015 Assessment (market price may be higher)	Average Rent for two bedroom apartment
Prince Rupert	$229,000	$794
Terrace	$317,000	$833
Kitimat	$316,000	$1,200[2]
Smithers	$276,000	$850[3]
Prince George	$251,000	$771
Fort St. John	$376,000	$1,077
Dawson Creek	$264,000	$1,120
Fort Nelson	$272,000	$934[4]
Northern Average	$257,000	$947

Average house price source: BC Assessment 2015 Assessment News Releases

Average rent source: CMHC Rental Market Report, British Columbia Highlights, Fall 2014

A Healthy Place for Children

Alex Pietralla grew up in Central Europe and has lived in Terrace since 2009.

What are the benefits of living in the Northwest?

Certainly cost of living. Then, these small communities offer a lot of family values. I grew up in a smaller community myself and I came home from school, I ate something, and then for the next five hours I wasn't seen again; I was somewhere playing. And this is how my son grows up – it's the same idea. It's a very healthy way of growing up. We feel very safe here too.

It's quieter and away from the hustle and bustle. I don't lose anywhere between four and six hours a week in a traffic jam just sitting in my car. That adds a lot of quality to life. I can have lunch at home with my wife sometimes. These are great things to have. I lived in a big city. I lived the hustle and bustle and when you don't have them you kind of lose touch with the quality to it. And I think that people here are very in tune and in touch with nature because it's so predominant and around them.

Education

Post-secondary

Training is essential for most businesses, since the competitive landscape and technology are constantly changing. The provincial government, under pressure from major industries worried about getting the workforce they need, has begun to focus on improving post-secondary facilities, particularly for the trades. All of the Northern post-secondary institutions offer courses in supervisory skills, project management, and other business related training through their continuing education programs.

Post-secondary options have been increasing in the North since 1990, when the University of Northern British Columbia (UNBC) opened in Prince George. Since then, the University has expanded its options and now students can earn degrees in nursing, medicine, and engineering as well as MBAs, all while remaining in the region. UNBC has campuses in most of the major towns and cities in the North, including Terrace, Quesnel, and Fort St. John.

College education is also available. Northern Lights College has its main campus in Fort St. John. Given its proximity to major natural gas fields, the College specializes in training for the natural gas industry and related trades.

The College also has campuses in Fort Nelson and Dawson Creek.

Northwest Community College (NWCC) has its main campus in Terrace, with smaller campuses in Prince Rupert, Smithers, and Hazelton. NWCC, after years of neglect, is getting a new $30 million trades building on its Terrace campus. In addition, its Smithers campus has a well-respected program focusing on mining exploration.

In the Prince George area, the College of New Caledonia offers mining, construction, and forestry training programs. From 2015 to 2018, it will be rolling out instructor-led video lectures to classrooms across multiple CNC campuses in the central region of British Columbia.

All three colleges provide trades and apprenticeship training programs. Individual college websites provide information on program offerings and the Trades Training BC website (Tradestrainingbc.ca) lists training schedules and availability of seats.

Elementary and Secondary Schooling

School children in British Columbia generally score well in international math and English competitions. In the 2012 Program for International Student Assessment, among 65 countries, BC students came in sixth in reading and science and 12th in math. The provincial government allocates about 26 per cent of its budget to education. Aboriginal students are finishing high school at an increasing rate (up to over 60 per cent in 2014, an increase of 18 per cent since 2001). Generally, most children study in well-equipped facilities with good teachers. Teachers in the province are well respected globally and throughout Canada. A BC teacher can often move anywhere in the country and have their credentials recognized, which is not true of all provinces. A teacher from Ontario or Quebec will often have to upgrade their education to be certified in British Columbia.

Secondary schools in the North have developed some particularly innovative programs. In the Northeast, the respected Northern Opportunities Program brings together schools and major industry to encourage high school students to begin studying for trades and other careers. Many graduate from high school with their training completed and can move quickly into highly paid jobs.

High School Success: The Northern Opportunities Program

The Northern Opportunities™ Partnership (NOP) began in 2002 as an industry-led initiative. Projected shortages of skilled labour in Northeast BC motivated industry to create a strategy to fill the gap. NOP took high school dual-credit programs to another level by providing students with personalized learning.

NOP partners include:

- BC Hydro
- Northern Lights College
- British Columbia Institute of Technology
- Canadian Natural Resources Limited
- Canfor Corporation
- Spectra Energy
- Encana Corporation
- Shell Canada
- Northern Development Initiative Trust
- North East Native Advancing Society
- Chalo School

In grades 10 through 12, students complete courses, dual credit programs, and/or apprenticeships. NOP helps students to earn post-secondary credit early, and to get a head start on their post-secondary education, training, and career. NOP's statistics demonstrate success in substantially increasing dual credit completion and Grade 12 graduation results, especially for Aboriginal students. In regular programs, 53 per cent of Aboriginal students graduate. In contrast, 79 per cent of participants in dual credit programs graduate.

Shopping

As outlined in Chapter 2, many opportunities exist to provide enhanced retail services in Northern British Columbia. Most communities have shops that offer basic groceries and food stuffs, hardware, and sporting goods. Some towns act as service centres for large areas: Terrace in the Northwest, Prince George in Central BC, and Fort St. John in the Northeast. Terrace and Fort St. John have Canadian Tire franchises and Wal-Mart stores, while Prince George also has a Costco Warehouse.

Many residents of smaller towns will travel to Prince George, Vancouver, or Edmonton to make major purchases. Dawson Creek retailers must contend with shoppers heading to Alberta, where there is no provincial sales tax, in contrast to the seven per cent tax that British Columbia levies. Internet shopping is also popular.

Health Care

Even the smallest towns in the North generally have some sort of clinic. Larger communities have hospitals that meet many regional needs. Prince George is home to the BC Cancer Agency Centre for the North, a full service cancer treatment and university teaching hospital. Fort St. John opened a new $300 million hospital in 2012, which includes an intensive care unit and birthing centre.

Like many rural areas, a challenge for smaller northern towns is to find physicians and other health professionals willing to be locally-based. In 2014, communities like Fort St. John, Dawson Creek, Fort Nelson, Burns Lake, and Chetwynd faced a particular lack of doctors. The provincial government offers cash incentives, the Northern Health Authority recruits aggressively, and the University of Northern BC has a medical program, but doctor shortages remain an ongoing problem in many places. Professions in high demand throughout the North are specialty nurses, occupational and physical therapists, and professionals in related health fields.

In 2014, the *Prince George Citizen* newspaper ran a series on the shortage of rural surgeons and the increased requirement for trauma and surgical patients to be transferred outside the region. A typical example is that of an expectant mother who may require a Caesarean section. Often, she must travel to Prince George or Vancouver to await the birth of her baby.

This health care situation is improving over time. Nonetheless, if you or a family member have health issues or are responsible for aging parents, you should investigate health care options in a community prior to moving there.

After Work Activities: Community Life

One question people often have when moving to a new place is, "So, what is there to do after work?" I've found that northern communities are active and engaged. With cultural and ethnic clubs, numerous sports leagues, social clubs for youth and seniors, and community volunteer groups, you'll find northern communities are lively places. They offer plenty of activities for singles, couples, and families. In fact, it's the after work lifestyle that attracts so many people to the region.

In smaller communities, you have no need to worry about traffic jams or road rage. Commutes are generally short, communities are close-knit, and you have more time to spend on leisure activities or with your family. You can get to know your neighbours.

Small-town life doesn't mean you have to sacrifice urban amenities, however—many northern communities have cafes, restaurants, theatres, and unique shops—and there's almost always free parking!

Why I Love Fort Nelson

Laurie Dolan is the Campus Administrator of Northern Lights College and a Councillor with the Northern Rockies Regional Municipality.

What do you like best about living in the North?

The lifestyle – it's very positive. I think Fort Nelson is a fantastic place. It has such a community sense about it. Our volunteer population is huge. We have a lot of not-for-profit organizations: such as the Literacy Society, the Hospital Foundation, the Seniors' Society. You see important projects get done mainly because the community is just so committed and always paying back.

The cost of living here is really affordable. People are sometimes shocked when they come here, especially those who are not fond of the oil and gas industry. They come up here and think there will be dead birds and trees, but much of the community is very holistic and I think that's just the northern way. If you need exercise, you can get out and walk in 40 below; that's not a problem.

We have a health food store here that won the BC Hydro green award for all of BC. It's the greenest manufactured building north of Prince George and they do a booming business. The majority of the community is definitely health conscious; they have access to organic vegetables and fruit and we have farmers that raise organic beef and chicken.

Sporting facilities are quite good across the North and are well used. (I swim regularly when I travel and have tried the pools in almost every town.) Most communities have newer swimming pools, ice and curling rinks, and plenty of soccer and baseball fields. Many have organized sports teams for children, men, and women, with enthusiastic participation. Fans of ice hockey will generally have a local junior team to cheer on. If you're a golfer, there's likely a course nearby.

In February 2015, Prince George, with Host First Nation the Lheidli T'enneh, welcomed about 15,000 visitors for the Canada Winter Games, a pan-Canadian sporting event. This event was the largest multi-sport and cultural event to ever be held in Northern British Columbia. The City was left with an Olympic-size hockey rink, upgraded community centres, and a Nordic ski centre with trails that meet national standards.

As mentioned, communities will usually have various cultural organizations, including theatre and arts groups. It's unrealistic to expect the caliber of the Beijing Opera or London's West End, but the North is not a wasteland either. Prince George has a symphony orchestra and two professional theatre companies. Various singers and rock bands head North frequently with shows that draw fans from across the region.

Northern British Columbia has a rich history that shows itself in community events, the arts, and a wide variety of festivals. First Nations culture as well as theatre, dance, music, and visual arts from all over the world play a part in the North's arts scene. Northerners enjoy a party, so exhibitions and other community events abound year round. Some of the more popular ones include:

- Fort Nelson—Trapper's Rendezvous (Winter Festival)
- Fort St. John—High on Ice Festival
- Dawson Creek—Dawson Creek Exhibition and Stampede
- Kitimat—Labour Day Fishing Derby
- Prince Rupert—All Native Basketball Tournament
- Terrace—Riverboat Days
- Smithers—Bulkley Valley Exhibition
- Prince George—British Columbia Northern Exhibition

The Outdoors

The North is beautiful. In the words of Stephen Hume:

It includes the prairies of the Peace River district, the glittering summit of Mount Fairweather in the St. Elias Mountains, the lava flows of the Spatsizi Plateau and the Nass Valley, the Northern Rockies that have been dubbed the Serengeti of the North for their abundance of wildlife and the craggy shores and fog-draped rainforests of Haida Gwaii, which droops down to roughly the same latitude as Williams Lake.

The snowpack and glaciers on seven major mountain ranges provide the meltwater that seethes through vast watersheds to form some of the continent's most powerful and dramatic rivers. They carve through the volcanic, mineral-rich bedrock. It was the floury dust, flakes and nuggets of placer gold these rivers deposited in gravel bars that made the North the transformative engine in B.C.'s economic and social history.[5]

If you like the outdoors, you'll love the North. In the spring and summer the countryside is gorgeous. The natural beauty of the region creates an inspiring backdrop for outdoor activities. You can experience it first-hand while biking, hiking, camping, or just exploring. The rivers and lakes that traverse the region offer excellent fishing, boating, and canoeing. In coastal communities like Kitimat and Prince Rupert, you also have the option of water sports on the Pacific Ocean. (See the photos at the start of this book for some examples of Northern landscapes.)

There's plenty of ice and snow in the winter and northerners make the most of it. Generally, cross-country skiing, dog sledding, and snowshoeing are all available and many towns have hundreds of kilometers of snowmobile trails, often through breathtaking landscapes. In Northeastern towns, you can watch the beautiful northern lights. There are downhill skiing hills in some communities; popular spots include Hudson Bay in Smithers, or Powder King in Prince George.

In the North, you'll have numerous opportunities to view bears, eagles, moose, deer, and other wildlife. If you are so inclined (and have the proper course accreditation, tags, and permits), you can also hunt them. On the coast, wildlife includes whales, seals, and other sea mammals.

Services for New Canadians

The North has traditionally had lower levels of immigration than the rest of British Columbia. With more Temporary Foreign workers arriving, however, particularly in the Northeast, towns are becoming more diverse. In years past, waves of immigrants made their homes in the North including:

- Vietnamese in Prince Rupert
- Portuguese in Kitimat
- Punjabis in Prince George
- And since the mid-2000s, Filipinos in Fort St. John and Fort Nelson

Faith and cultural organizations serving a wide range of immigrant communities are also active in the region. Again, numbers are smaller than in a large metropolitan centre, but they are growing.

Most towns offer programs for community integration, language training, and settlement assistance through robust literacy and diversity societies. School districts or local colleges offer language training programs. Some communities have larger programs, like S.U.C.C.E.S.S. in Fort St. John, which is a branch office of the large immigrant settlement society that has been in Vancouver for over 25 years (www.successbc.ca).

The provincial government funds the Skills Connect for Immigrants Program. This initiative helps permanent residents find jobs and will offer industry specific skills training and language skill upgrading. Offices of the program are located in Fort St. John, Prince George, and Prince Rupert.

Summary

British Columbia's North is a vast region and travel, especially in winter, can be daunting. Preparation and planning at any time is important, since as the economy grows, demand for travel-related goods and services often outstrips supply. Living in the North has its own rhythm, advantages, and challenges. Communities have more cultural and civic amenities than many people from outside realize and programs for newcomers are increasing. As for life after work, there's lots to do, especially if you love the outdoors.

CHAPTER 6

The New North
A Business Roadmap

The only way around is through.

Robert Frost

This chapter is designed to help you set up or expand your firm in British Columbia's North, focusing on information especially relevant to doing business in this region. If you are new to business and need more introductory information about starting a company, visit Small Business BC (smallbusinessbc.ca).

Researching Target Communities

You're considering establishing or buying an existing business in a particular town or region. Some first steps likely include conducting market research, exploring commercial real estate options, and so forth. To speed up the process and get the most current information, consider connecting with one or more of the following:

- **Economic development offices**—Many communities have an economic development officer (EDO) who works extensively with businesses. The Appendices contain a list of contacts for Aboriginal and major community offices current as of June 2015. EDOs generally have access to a treasure-trove of statistics, socio-economic profiles, and other data of commercial interest. They can alert you to government funding sources and programs that may be useful for helping with employee training. They'll have contacts within the town or city's planning department who can inform you about zoning requirements and any necessary permits you'll need (e.g. building, signage). Community Futures offices have good community information and business resources and may have a list of businesses for sale.

- **Chambers of Commerce**—Most major towns and cities have Chambers of Commerce, whose purpose is to support and promote local business. Their staff can be quite knowledgeable, since some may have lived in the community for years. Chambers often hold luncheons and other events that can be wonderful occasions to network with other businesses.

- **Service clubs**—The Rotary Club and other business clubs have chapters across the North. They hold luncheons and community events that are informative and provide an informal place to make connections and learn about business prospects. (Rotary Club members helped me make many useful contacts with companies when I was researching and interviewing for this book.)

- **Real estate brokers**—Good commercial real estate brokers have their finger on the pulse of the local economy. You will likely use their services when you are looking to rent, buy, or develop a property. Take advantage of their knowledge of the local business scene even before you decide to set up. If you are in the market to buy an existing business operation, brokers may be aware of business-owners looking to sell.

- **Accounting firms**—Larger communities will probably have an accounting firm or two. These professionals (and lawyers who specialize in this area) can be helpful if you're considering the purchase of an existing business. Through their work for various clients, they are often aware, informally, of owners wishing to sell. If you already have an accountant outside the community, he or she may be able to provide you with a referral. If not, set up an appointment with a firm in the target location, making your purpose clear. A local firm may also have detailed knowledge of various government financial programs and incentives specifically targeted to northern businesses.

- **Other non-competitive businesses**—Business people in the North can often be friendlier than those in large cities and many are quite civic-minded. They want a strong local economy and encourage commercial growth, so if you're not a direct competitor, they can offer some good advice. Ask an economic development officer, service club member, or Chamber staff member for potential referrals. Alternately, you can contact business owners directly and ask for 20 minutes of their time.

Accessing Capital

Many start-up businesses need capital, as do existing companies seeking to expand or improve their operations. Banks and credit unions are traditional sources of lending and many have branches in the major northern communities. Some other sources of capital listed below may be less familiar to you, but could provide the funding needed to move your firm to the next level.

- **Community Futures** (cfdc.bc.ca)—Supported by the federal government, Community Futures offices are located around the North. They specialize in small business lending and as their website notes:

  > Unlike most financial institutions, we are not a formula lender. Instead we assess every business venture on the basis of its own merit. Community Futures also has the ability to explore financing for businesses that are unable to secure funding under reasonable terms and conditions from traditional lenders. In some cases we may be prepared to consider a position of higher risk than other lenders.

- **Venture Capital Programs**—The provincial government has several programs to encourage investors to invest in BC small businesses that will "enhance and diversify the provincial economy." One eligible category is for "Community diversification outside of the Lower Mainland and Capital Region." A company using this category must also promote community diversification within the region. The types of businesses the program supports includes: manufacturing and processing, destination tourist resorts, research and development of proprietary technology, development of interactive digital media, clean technologies, non-traditional agricultural activities, and retail and commercial services. Learn more at the website of the Ministry of International Trade. (www.mit.gov.bc.ca)

Private venture capitalists and angel investors are another source of capital.

- **Crowdfunding**—Crowdfunding is by definition, "the practice of funding a project or venture by raising many small amounts of money from a large number of people, typically via the Internet." Well-known crowdfunding sites include Kickstarter (www.kickstarter.com), Indiegogo (www.indiegogo.com), and Fundrazr (fundrazr.com), which is based in British Columbia. Lots of others exist and their numbers are increasing – you can find many listed on the National Crowdfunding Association of Canada's website (ncfacanada.org). While each site offers their unique spin, the general concept is the same. Project creators develop a profile typically containing a short video, an introduction to their project, a list of rewards per donation, and some images. The idea is to create a compelling message to draw in readers. Many companies then launch social-media campaigns to promote their project through avenues such as Twitter or Facebook. Supporters make their contributions via PayPal, credit card, or other online options through the portal.

Start-up businesses and growing companies are increasingly exploring equity crowdfunding. In this variation, individual investors fund small businesses online in return for equity. In May 2015, the BC Securities Commission announced rules to govern Internet equity crowdfunding in the province. Learn more at www.bcsc.bc.ca. A site specializing in crowdfunding is Seattle-based InvestorNextDoor (www.investnextdoor.com), an equity crowdlending platform for small businesses that uses a peer-to-business model. The firm's goal is to provide up to $100,000 in reasonably priced capital to small businesses. Each peer lender benefits from returns that are structured as fixed income securities, with a 5 to 20 per cent return.

Government Funding Programs

Canada/BC Job Grant—Cost sharing program that helps employers off-set the cost of training for new or current employees. Employers can receive up to two-thirds of the cost of training to a maximum of $10,000 per grant. Turnaround on applications is estimated to be 30 days.

NDIT Competitive Consulting Rebate—Provides manufacturers and resource sector supply chain companies with management consulting expertise to expand operations, improve processes, and get certifications. The rebate is half the cost (50 per cent), with up to $30,000 available per company.

NDIT Northern Industry Expansion Program

a) A loan guarantee program with Business Development Bank of Canada (BDC) to extend financing capital. It's available to the resource, manufacturing, and supply sectors to support expansion plans – for equipment, building, and working capital. The guarantee can cover 25 per cent, up to $1 million.

b) A loan guarantee program with the National Bank. It provides purchase order financing to the resource, manufacturing, and supply sectors for materials and inventory to start the project. Receivables financing is available once work is completed and an invoice is generated. The guarantee can cover 25 per cent up to $1 million.

Women's Enterprise Centre (www.womensenterprise.ca)—Provides loans, business counseling, and skills training specifically for women entrepreneurs.

Finding and Keeping Staff: The Northern Challenge

In October 2014, the Prince George Chamber of Commerce released the results of a member survey that identified top priorities and issues facing local businesses. Many companies indicated they wanted to expand, but faced challenges related to recruitment and retention of talent. In fact, this human resources issue was their top strategic priority; specifically, recruitment and retention of *skilled* labour was seen as a major impediment to doing business in Prince George.[1]

Prince George is not alone in facing these staffing issues. Since the early 2000s, the Northeast has been at near full employment and certain types of skilled workers are in continual high demand. In 2014, Northwest British Columbia recorded the second highest job growth in BC, after the Lower Mainland, gaining 4,200 new positions.[2] The unemployment rate in all BC regions in 2014 was under six per cent which meant that labour was in demand and so it was harder to fill many jobs – and keep people in them.

In the North, local economies go through boom and bust cycles, with good and bad times sometimes lasting for years at a time. In the Northeast in 2013, Fort Nelson faced a downturn. It had lost its forest industry. As well, businesses were waiting on agreements with the companies involved in Liquefied Natural Gas. Tumbler Ridge lost their coal mines at the same time - their only industry other than tourism. Other areas in the Northeast continued to boom.[3] While jobs were plentiful in the Northwest in 2014, in the 2000s, the region endured years of double digit unemployment after the shut-down of sawmills and fish canneries. Prince George once faced similar cyclical patterns, but the addition of a university and more health care facilities has brought greater diversity and thus stability to the local economy. If you're planning to do business in the North for the long term, you need to account for these up and down periods in your business and human resources planning.

Another labour consideration is the aging provincial and national workforce. Many older employees, especially in skilled trades and technical and management positions, will be retiring between 2015 and 2020. Fact: it is going to be tougher to find skilled workers in the future. Companies adept at recruitment and retention will have a competitive advantage.

Some Recruitment Basics

If you're in an area of low unemployment, you will compete to hire and keep employees. Recruitment costs time and money, so it is important to do it well. The following pages have some suggestions to help attract good people who will stay with your company beyond a couple of pay periods, which, as northern employers told me, can be a problem when economies are hot!

Photo: Michael Ford Photography

- **Set pay and benefits at market rates**—Yes, it's true that salary is not everything, but if your offer is below the norm for your area, job-seekers will likely look elsewhere. Assess your local market and match the going rate.

- **Develop a good job description**—Think about the tasks associated with a position and the kinds of skills and attitudes of workers you've had in the past who were successful in the role. Also consider any essential certificates (e.g. safety-related) that a potential employee must have. The Appendices contain a sample job description for a construction worker and some potential interview questions.

- **Highlight the career advantages of the North**—According to a Rand Canada study released in April 2015, nearly one in five British Columbians are looking for a new job - with opportunity for career growth (not money) as the number one motivation.[4] As employers repeatedly mentioned to me, a major advantage of a northern career is the opportunity it provides for junior staff to take on tasks that would normally go to more senior colleagues in larger centres.

- **Highlight the benefits of living in the North**—A career in the North can be attractive to people if they know more about the region. Feature the advantages that northern living has to offer in your job posting. Include enticers such as access to:

  - More career opportunities and the potential for quicker advancement

  - Affordable housing in some communities (Fort St. John and Kitimat can be expensive places to buy or rent.)

  - The amenities of city life without all the hassles—no traffic and low parking fees! Shorter commutes mean more time to spend with family, friends, and neighbours

  - Year round outdoor activities, including a variety of eco-tourism day trips

- Good recreation facilities

- Arts and cultural activities such as local theatre shows, festivals, concerts, and other special events

- Friendly people with a strong sense of community

- **Include two or more people in the hiring decision**—It's helpful to invite a supervisor or a potential co-worker to interviews. These people will have to work with the candidate and may be able to quickly determine if he or she has the requisite knowledge and skills needed for the job. Perhaps more importantly, your hiring colleagues are in a better position to determine "fit" or suitability, picking up on personality subtleties that can make or break a team.

Program Supports Employment for People with Disabilities

A new program is available to people who have disabilities and their employers to assist them with maximizing their efforts at work. The Technology@Work Program is offered through the not-for-profit Neil Squire Society and is designed to:

- support employment for people with disabilities in British Columbia who are currently or just about to start working, are self-employed, or volunteering;

- provide eligible assistive technology, products, and services to individuals who have work and volunteer related barriers; and to

- offer services to individuals and employers.

For more information about the Technology@Work Program, visit the Neil Squire website (www.neilsquire.ca).

Initiatives Prince George Newsletter, May 2015

- **Create and maintain a positive workplace culture**—Job satisfaction is key to employee retention. When job opportunities are plentiful, employees are more inclined to "vote with their feet" leaving toxic or oppressive workplaces with little hesitation. Think about tangible and intangible incentives to support and nurture employees such as training and advancement opportunities, a collaborative work environment where employees are valued for different perspectives, and the active promotion of work-life balance.

Going beyond family and friends: Tapping into Labour Pools

You can access different sources of labour when recruiting employees for your business. Below are some well-known and less obvious sources of new staff.

Current Staff/Canadians living elsewhere

If your business is already established elsewhere, current staff members may be willing to relocate to the North. You might also consider general recruitment within Canada, looking to provinces where unemployment is higher.

Some northern communities are actively pursuing this option. Prince George has developed a website, *Move-Up Prince George*, (moveupprincegeorge.ca) which outlines the benefits of living in the city, along with job opportunities. The site provides information for potential employees on such topics as real estate, the rental market, amenities, schools, and health care. As the Chamber of Commerce notes, employers can list the *Move Up Prince George* website URL on job postings and on company websites. Other communities are developing similar materials; check out the community's website or Chamber of Commerce for materials and ideas.

Aboriginal Peoples

Depending on the location of the business, Aboriginal Peoples are another potential labour source. As outlined in Chapters Two and Three, many First Nations communities have a large cohort of young people. Unemployment rates on some reserves can be as high as eighty per cent. As outlined in Chapter Four, if you're bidding on major projects, you may have to consider partnering with Aboriginal firms and potentially hiring Aboriginal workers.

If you're new to Aboriginal recruitment, many communities in Northern British Columbia have Aboriginal employment societies or associations that can assist; some have online job boards. Examples of such organizations are:

- *Prince George:* The Prince George Nechako Aboriginal Employment and Training Association (PGNAETA) (pgnaeta.bc.ca)

- *Fort St. John/Fort Nelson:* Northeast Native Advancing Society (NENAS) (www.nenas.org)

- *Prince Rupert*: TRICORP's (tricorp.ca) mandate is to provide financing for business activities among First Nations people. It also has good contacts with Aboriginal job-seekers.

- *Aboriginal Friendship Centres* (www.bcaafc.com/bc-friendship-centres) are community centres that often have employment officers who collect and advertise job postings to Aboriginal job seekers. Friendship Centres can be found in Terrace, Smithers, Prince George, Fort St. John, Chetwynd, Dawson Creek, and Fort Nelson.

For helpful background reading on hiring Aboriginal employees, try online resources like:

- ECO Canada's *Aboriginal Recruitment Guide* (www.eco.ca/pdf/Aboriginal-Recruitment-Guide.pdf)

Your next best sustainable natural resource – the Aboriginal Workforce

With a long term, supportive, and holistic approach to employment and training practices, your organization can benefit richly from a willing and nearby resource pool. The Aboriginal Workforce is not only available, and local, but is also your next best sustainable natural resource development opportunity.

Top 7 Sustainable Training Practices

1. Case management support in local communities (includes post-employment support
2. Pre-acceptance in-community drug and alcohol testing (voluntary)
3. Assistance with social insurance numbers
4. Driver's licence training
5. Safety ticket training
6. Interventions as needed
7. Job readiness training (may include pre-industry employment)

Top 7 Sustainable Hiring Practices

1. Culturally appropriate Human Resources policies and practices including diversity training
   a. Cultural celebrations within the workplace
   b. Organizational participation in community events
   c. Culturally appropriate leave mechanisms
   d. Peer mentorship
   e. 1-800 on-call culturally appropriate support available 24/7

2. Hiring in pairs and multiples

3. Transportation to and from the work site

4. Provision of on-site accommodation

5. Provision of Personal Protective Equipment

6. Available on-site child care

7. Active support and recognition of the employee's family at home

Sandra Sutter, the Aboriginal Partnerships Manager for Tarpon Energy Services, and the Circle for Aboriginal Relations' Business Manager, is the Co-Chair of the Métis Women's Economic Security Council for Alberta Aboriginal Relations. She is actively involved in the Friendship Centre Movement, serving at local and national levels. Many of the insights listed above are based on the work of a three year pilot project with Enform, the Federation of Saskatchewan Indian Nations, Battlefords Agency Tribal Chiefs, and File Hills Qu'Appelle Development Corporation. She can be reached at sandra@sandrasutter.com.

- StepUp BC's online toolkit, *Hiring Aboriginal Employees*, which includes links to Aboriginal focused employment sites (stepupbc. ca/develop-your-non-profit-recruitment-and-hiring/hiring-aboriginal-employees-overview#.VSmq3_nF_To).

Although these guides target particular sectors (environmental and non-profit), they both contain excellent advice and resources for employers in all industries.

- The Alberta government's *Finding and Keeping Aboriginal Employees A Handbook for Small and Medium-sized Businesses* (2009), while older, still has numerous helpful tips and provides sound advice.

Unions/Recruitment Agencies

For skilled trades, unions can be a source of labour, since they have access to large pools of trained workers.[5] Some unions offer the ability to set up a collective bargaining agreement between the contractor and union to govern work conditions and wage rates that is effective only until a specifically named project is completed. British Columbia has two major construction unions: the BC Building Trades (representing 12 construction related unions) and Christian Labour Association of Canada (CLAC).

Another possibility is to use a recruitment agency. With the rising demand for skilled workers in the North, companies are establishing satellite offices in northern communities. They deal with companies of all sizes and may be a fast way to find an employee in a crunch or a highly skilled professional unavailable locally. In Kitimat, a private training college, Kitimat Valley Institute, operates an active industrial recruiting agency.

New Canadians or permanent residents from Metro Vancouver

The vast majority of immigrants to British Columbia first settle in Metro Vancouver. In 2010, for example, almost 80 per cent indicated that they intended to reside in the region.[6] Some have difficulties finding a job appropriate to their skill levels in a crowded and competitive labour market. The North, with its low unemployment rate and numerous jobs, could be an attractive alternative as a new home. People who have immigrated to Canada, and in particular to British Columbia, might consider heading north if the right opportunity is presented.

The idea of attracting recent immigrants to the North has been gaining in popularity. In 2013, my company, Ingenia, partnered with the Kitimat Chamber of Commerce to pilot workshops in nine northern communities. The half-day sessions were designed to inform small business employers about the option and benefits of hiring new Canadians. The pilot was a success.

As a result of the pilot, local Chambers of Commerce, in concert with the Immigrant Employment Council of BC, began offering workshops showcasing the benefits of employing immigrants and encouraging companies to hire them. In a March 2015 media release, Initiatives Prince George states:

In recognition of the current demand for skilled professionals in central and northern BC communities, the Immigrant Employment Council of BC (IEC-BC) launched an initiative to connect employers in Prince George, Prince Rupert, and Fort St. John to new Canadians in Metro Vancouver.

A dynamic website - www.northernbcjobs.com - featuring Northern BC employment opportunities and job networking resources has been developed, and is being promoted through digital, print, and broadcast advertising, video and collateral materials such as posters, an employer toolkit, and promo cards, and social media and media relations.[7]

If you think new Canadians might be an answer to your hiring needs, you can advertise your job opportunities to them through:

- **Local immigrant serving agencies**—Most communities have a diversity or literacy society. Often new Canadians looking for work in a town will visit these organizations to make contacts. For example, they might stop at the Immigrant and Multicultural Services Society (IMSS) of Prince George or the Fort Nelson Community Literacy Society. Or, newcomers may search for work at local employment service agencies, the offices of WORKBC (located throughout the province), or Hecate Strait Employment Development Society in Prince Rupert or Employment Connections in Fort St. John, all which provide specific employment services for immigrants.

- **Referrals from workers or employers**—If you have a new Canadian staff member, he or she may be able to recommend other workers. Employers in the community who have successfully hired new Canadians may also have recruitment suggestions.

- **Immigrant agencies in the Lower Mainland**—Two of the major immigrant serving agencies are S.U.C.C.E.S.S. (www.successbc.ca) and Mosaic (www.mosaicbc.com). These Vancouver-based organizations give regular employment seminars to internationally trained professionals and hold job fairs in the Lower Mainland. S.U.C.C.E.S.S. also has an office in Fort St. John. Contacting these agencies and indicating your hiring needs can be a good first step.

- **Advertise in ethnic media**—The Vancouver area has many newspapers catering to people of various ethnic backgrounds, some published in English and others in different languages. Consider placing an ad in one of them. You can even have your English ad translated into Mandarin or Punjabi (Google has an increasingly accurate service) and have it published in a Chinese or Indo-Canadian newspaper. Don't shy away from marketing employment opportunities in a foreign language paper for fear that their readers have weak English. In fact, many new Canadians with good English read papers in their native language, seeking the latest news from back home.

Of interest to newcomers, some communities already have established immigrant communities. These include Vietnamese in Prince Rupert, Punjabis in Prince George, and Filipinos and Sikhs in Fort St. John.

Hiring from Outside of Canada: The Immigration Game

You may be unsuccessful getting the staff you need from Canada and may have to consider engaging workers from another country. This section highlights major federal and provincial immigration programs of interest to business.

Federal Immigration Programs

Since 2006, the federal government has focused on attracting immigrants who can help meet labour market shortages and fill skills gaps. In its 2015 Immigration Levels Plan, Citizenship and Immigration, (CIC), the federal department responsible for some aspects of immigration, pledged to accept 260,000 to 285,000 new permanent residents. About two-thirds would be economic immigrants.[8]

The Canadian government has three long-standing programs designed to bring in economic immigrants:

1. **Federal Skilled Worker Program (FSWP)** is designed to attract immigrants who possess skills and capabilities that enable them to quickly integrate and begin to contribute to the Canadian labour market. The government assesses applicants based on various criteria including education, work experience, age, English and/or French language abilities, adaptability, and other factors. The FSWP remains the largest source of economic immigrants for Canada and BC.

2. **Federal Skilled Trades Program (FSTP)** helps employers find skilled trades people and is structured similarly to the Skilled Worker Program. The FSTP puts more emphasis on practical training and work experience than formal education. To qualify, an immigrant must have:

   - At least two years' full-time experience in their trade within the previous five years.

   - An offer of full-time employment for at least one year OR have a certificate of qualification in that skilled trade issued by a provincial or territorial body.

   - Intermediate Language skills: All applicants must take a language proficiency test in reading, writing, speaking, and listening.

   - No criminal record or health issues for the applicant OR family members.

   - An ability to support themselves and their families. Workers must disclose their assets and liabilities, and the amount of "settlement funds" available. The amount required will vary based on family size.

   In 2014, 90 occupations were eligible for this program, including industrial, electrical, and construction trades and maintenance and equipment operations trades. Also qualified were supervisors and technical occupations in natural resources, processing, and manufacturing, as well as utility supervisors, central control operators, chefs, bakers, and butchers.

For companies wanting to use the FSTP, there is a catch to the offer of employment. An employer cannot simply make a job offer and expect the worker to be on the next plane to Canada. The process, alas, is time consuming and labour intensive. Companies must first apply to Service Canada for a positive "Labour Market Impact Assessment" (LMIA). This positive LMIA (sometimes called a confirmation letter) attests that a need exists for a foreign worker to fill the job and that no Canadian is available.

To get a positive LMIA, you have to advertise the position in Canada, offering the "median wage." If these efforts fail to uncover a suitable Canadian, you can then apply for the LMIA. You will have to provide numerous supporting documents to Service Canada, including business documentation (such as licenses and income tax information).

Even if you navigate successfully through this LMIA step, getting the employee to Canada can take months, depending on where the person is coming from. The estimated time to navigate the entire process can range from months to years.

3. **Canadian Experience Class (CEC)** is for people who already have skilled work experience in Canada and want to immigrate permanently. Some high-skilled temporary foreign workers can use this class. For many international university graduates, the CEC offers the fastest and simplest route to achieving permanent residence. After completing a program or course of study at a Canadian educational institution, some students are able to remain in Canada on post-graduate work permits. If, during this time, they obtain a minimum of one year of work in a skilled, professional or technical field, they may then become eligible to enter the Express Entry Program under the Canadian Experience Class. (See the following pages for more information on Express Entry.)

Faster recognition of foreign credentials

Once in Canada, many immigrants have trouble getting their credentials recognized, so that they can work in the occupation they trained for. In response to this challenge, the Canadian government has improved the speed at which foreign credentials are recognized for 24 priority occupations. Among these are geoscientists, carpenters, electricians, heavy duty equipment technicians, heavy equipment operators, welders, and engineers. Through this initiative, internationally trained professionals have their qualifications assessed within one year and are eligible for microloans to help cover the cost.

Accessing Canada's Immigration Programs to Address Labour Shortages: What Employers Need to Know!

Catherine A. Sas Q.C.

Canadian employers have been challenged to fill pressing labour shortages for many years and the projections are that these shortages will continue for years to come. Nowhere will these be felt more acutely than in Northern Canada. Notwithstanding all the various opinions as to the best way to resolve our pressing shortage of workers, immigration is universally recognized as being essential to address Canada's immediate and long term labour force needs.

For employers seeking to resolve their labour shortages, it is becoming essential to navigate Canada's immigration programs to keep your workforce strong and your business thriving. Here's what you can do to master the immigration game!

Hot Tips for Employers

CONSIDER THE PROS AND CONS OF CANADA'S TEMPORARY VERSUS PERMANENT IMMIGRATION PROGRAMS

Generally the temporary processes are quicker and allow you to transition your workers to permanent residence status later.

BECOME FAMILIAR WITH SERVICE CANADA'S APPLICATION PROCESS FOR A LABOUR MARKET IMPACT ASSESSMENT (LMIA)

If you aren't up for navigating the process on your own – work with a skilled immigration professional: a licensed immigration lawyer or consultant.

TREAT SERVICE CANADA LIKE YOU WOULD REVENUE CANADA!

Be aware of the compliance measures for employers in Canada's immigration program. Penalties for non-compliant employers can be severe.

DO WHAT YOU SAY YOU ARE GOING TO DO!

Employers are legally obligated to honour the provisions of their offers of employment to employees made to Service Canada in LMIA applications and to CIC in work permit applications. Failure of an employer to comply with offered terms of employment may result in heavy fines and prohibition from employing foreign workers for a period of two years.

DEVELOP AN IMMIGRATION STRATEGY AND CREATE WRITTEN INTERNAL POLICIES FOR ALL FOREIGN WORKERS

Employers are now required to keep all immigration records for both Service Canada and CIC regarding ALL foreign workers for a period of six years. Service Canada and CIC may ask any employer to demonstrate that they have complied with the offered terms of employment for any foreign worker at ANY time. Employers need to have a system in place to be able to respond to a Compliance Audit request!

WORK WITH REPUTABLE RECRUITERS

Know that Service Canada and CIC deem employers to be responsible for the actions of the recruiters that they work with whether in Canada or overseas. Recruiters are prohibited from charging individual workers for finding them an employer in Canada!

CONSIDER THE WORKER PROVISIONS OF CANADA'S INTERNATIONAL TRADE AGREEMENTS:

Canada presently has international trade agreements with five countries (and is negotiating with many more!). Learn what types of occupations are covered under these agreements that allow for speedier processing.

EMPLOY INTERNATIONAL STUDENTS ON A PART TIME BASIS WHILE STUDYING AND FULL TIME AFTER GRADUATION:

Many international students are able to work part-time while studying and are eligible for open work permits after graduation for up to three years. There are also Permanent Residence options after gaining at least one year of work experience.

EMBRACE THE NEW **"EXPRESS ENTRY"** PROGRAM FOR FINDING WORKERS

Canada's "Express Entry" selection system is designed to match employers with suitable workers. Be sure to register as an employer when the JOB BANK matching program becomes operational in summer 2015.

KNOW YOUR IMMIGRATION PROFESSIONAL!

Canada's immigration laws stipulate who can provide immigration services for a fee. Only a lawyer licensed with a Canadian law society, a Notary in Quebec, or an Immigration consultant licensed with the Immigration Consultants of Canada Regulatory Council (ICCRC) are lawfully permitted to provide paid immigration services in dealing with the Government of Canada. Employers are responsible for complying with these rules even with foreign overseas immigration advisors.

Catherine Sas, QC has over 25 years of experience as an immigration lawyer. She provides a full range of immigration services and has been recognized as a leading immigration practitioner by Lexpert, Who's Who Legal and Best Lawyers in Canada. In 2014, Catherine was voted Vancouver's Best Immigration Lawyer for the third consecutive year. Catherine is also the co-author of "Immigrate to Canada – A Practical Guide" and also writes a monthly blog on her website www.canadian-visa-lawyer.com.

2015 Game Changer: Express Entry Program

For years, the Canadian immigration system operated on the basis of processing applications in the order received. With the Express Entry online program, established January 1, 2015, the federal government has set up a "just-in-time" immigration system, modelled after those of New Zealand and Australia. In the words of Jason Kenney, the federal Minister of Immigration in 2012:

> The new system, in part, will be based on what's called an expression of interest system. Newcomers from around the world will make an application online if they want to come to Canada. They'll fill out a basic form. And eventually, with that form, they'll have to attach a pre-assessment of their credentials that we will run by the national bodies representing the professional licensing organizations. Once they've done those pre-assessments, they'll go into a pool of applicants to share their applications with employers and with provinces that have Provincial Nominee Programs.
>
> In a practical sense, what does this mean? Employers will go online, register with (the immigration department), and do a search in that

pool of pre-qualified applicants, to look for the people who have the skills that he needs and have expressed an interest in coming to Canada. (The employer) can then contact them, do his due diligence, interview them on Skype, hire an overseas recruitment agency, do what he needs to do. And if he's satisfied with their skills, he can offer them the position. We verify the person's application, and then bring them here in (six) months.[9]

Instead of an applicant driven model, Express Entry is intended to be selection driven. The government will use the program to manage applications to the Federal Skilled Worker Program, Federal Skilled Trades Program, Canadian Experience Class, and a portion of the Provincial Nominee Program. Citizenship and Immigration Canada (CIC) describes the new system as follows:

- CIC selects candidates who are most likely to succeed in Canada, rather than the first in line.

- Express Entry candidates with a valid job offer or provincial nomination will quickly be *invited to apply* (ITA) for permanent residence.

- Later in 2015 the new Job Bank will connect Canadian employers with a pool of skilled foreign national candidates if they are unable to find Canadians or permanent residents to do the job.

- Processing times for Express Entry candidates will be six months or less.[10]

The government is still fine-tuning the program and likely will make more adjustments in response to labour market needs. For the most current information, visit the CIC website at www.cic.gc.ca.

Temporary Foreign Worker Program (TFWP)

Rather than go through the process of hiring a worker who will live in Canada permanently, many companies have been accessing the Temporary Foreign Worker Program (TFWP.) The TFWP allows employers to hire foreign workers to fill temporary labour and skill shortages. Employers may be able to hire eligible foreign workers to work temporarily if they can prove that:

- They cannot find suitable Canadians or permanent residents to fill the jobs,

- Bringing the workers to Canada will have no negative impact on the Canadian labour market, and

- They meet all other requirements and conditions.

Under the umbrella of this program, employers can hire workers abroad or currently in Canada. Examples of qualified foreign workers already in Canada include those about to complete a job contract with another employer or those holding an open work permit that allows them to work for any employer.

From 2006 onward, hundreds of thousands of temporary foreign workers (TFWs) entered the country. In British Columbia, there were 70,000 TFWs at the end of 2011.[11] Some towns in the North have also used TFWs extensively; in my travels to Fort St. John, Dawson Creek, and Fort Nelson, local employers at retail outlets, food stores, and gas stations told me that without temporary foreign workers, they would have almost no staff; one had hired eight TFWs to run his grocery store, another over a dozen to staff his retail outlet.

As the TFWP grew over time, so did the controversies associated with it. In 2012, in response to rising complaints from unions and others, the federal government introduced new rules to prevent businesses from abusing the TFWP. It limited to four the cumulative number of years a TFW could remain in Canada and tightened hiring regulations. Companies faced stiffer penalties for making illegitimate job offers and a permanent ban from the program if they broke the rules.

Temporary Foreign Worker Program (TFWP) changes explained[12]

The Canadian Federation of Independent Business (www.cfib-fcei.ca) summarized the June 2014 changes to the Temporary Foreign Worker Program in an online article, abridged below. The CFIB updates this information regularly.

Many changes could have negative impacts on Small and Medium Enterprises (SMEs):

- The government no longer accepts applications for low skilled workers in the accommodation, food services, and retail trade sectors in economic regions with an unemployment rate at or above six per cent.

- Many sectors and regions are completely excluded access to TFWP.

- Labour Market Impact Assessment applications for certain low skilled positions will no longer be accepted.

- The program no longer classifies low skilled workers by their occupation and skill level required, but by the hourly wage the job pays.

- Workers that are paid below the provincial median wage are now classified as low wage workers.

- As of April 2015, migrant workers who have been employed in Canada for four years or more must leave the country and cannot work in Canada for another four years, after which they can reapply for a work permit. As of July 2015, employers can have no more than 20 per cent of their workforce as low-wage temporary foreign workers. The number must drop to 10 per cent starting in July 2016.

Significantly higher costs to access TFWP:

- The LMIA application fee increased from $275 to $1,000 per position. Employment and Social Development Canada will also charge employers an additional $100 privilege fee.

- This LMIA fee is non-refundable, even if the LMIA is rejected.

Increased paperwork and regulations:

- Employers who wish to hire a TFW must first have gone through an extensive process to search for **Canadians able to do the job as advertised** in a public medium such as newspapers, job posting Internet site, bulletin boards, etc.

- Employers with 10 or more employees applying for a new LMIA are subject to a cap on low wage workers. This cap will be based on the number of full-time and part-time positions staffed by an employer at a specific work location. It has been set at 20 per cent as of July 1, 2015 and will decrease to 10 per cent as of July 1, 2016.

Despite the changes, by 2013, the outcry over the TFW Program and its administration was becoming louder. News programs featured stories of a firm in the Northeast advertising for miners who spoke Mandarin, of fast-food restaurants cutting back shifts of Canadian workers in favour of TFWs, and of a large bank laying off Canadian staff so that they could bring in lower cost TFWs from India. Other reports focused on employer abuses related to wages and accommodation for their foreign workers.

In June 2014, the federal government announced more adjustments to the TFW program. The major elements are outlined in the box that starts on the previous page. These changes have had a significant, largely negative impact on many small businesses and in particular the hospitality, retail, and restaurant sectors.

As noted earlier, some British Columbian companies rely heavily on TFWs and expected to lose a significant amount of low wage workers as a result of the program changes. On December 31, 2013, temporary foreign workers made up 0.93 per cent of the provincial labour force, in contrast to the national average of 0.55 per cent. After Alberta, British Columbia has the second highest reliance on temporary foreign workers of any province or territory. In 2016, when the limits on low-wage temporary foreign workers come into full effect, the number of entrants to British Columbia is expected to decrease by 2,362, accounting for 15 per cent of Canada's TFW reduction. Only Alberta will have lost more low-wage temporary foreign workers.[13]

Provincial Immigration Programs

British Columbia also has immigration programs of interest to employers in the North.

Provincial Nominee Program (PNP)

BC administers the PNP program under an agreement with the federal government called the Canada British Columbia Immigration Agreement. The Program allows employers to attract and retain economic immigrants by providing a pathway to permanent residency. The federal government allocates an annual quota of PNP nominations to each province, with British Columbia allowed to nominate 5,500 principal applicants in 2015. Nominees must either have an offer of job of indeterminate length from a BC employer, a master's or doctorate degree from a BC post-secondary institution in select fields, or be experienced entrepreneurs who are willing to invest in and actively manage a business in the province.

Under the PNP, the province establishes the selection criteria and nominates applicants for permanent residence. The federal government makes the final decision for permanent residence, determining admissibility on the basis of health, criminality, and security grounds. Prospective immigrants apply first to the provincial PNP to be selected (nomination) and then to the federal government to become Permanent Residents, along with their immediate family members.

As a business owner, it's important to note that education and language ability are particularly strong among PNP principal applicants and their families. In 2012, over 60 per cent of principal applicants had a university degree or higher. A further 28.8 per cent had a college education or trade certificate.

Between 2008 and 2013, the number of immigrants becoming residents of British Columbia through the PNP almost doubled from 3,628 to 7,128. (These figures include the principal applicants and their spouses and dependents.) In 2013, as has been the case since 2004, the top source countries of all immigrants were Mainland China, India, and the Philippines.

In March 2015, British Columbia announced it was revamping the PNP program, to streamline the application process and develop program criteria better suited to meeting labour market needs. (More practically, Temporary Foreign Workers seeking residence swamped the program with applications in early 2015. As a result, PNP application processing times jumped from three to 13 months.)[14] The government said that it would launch a revised and updated PNP in July 2015.

Northeast Pilot Project

The Northeast Pilot Project started in 2012 and has been extended until March 31, 2016. Through this Project, the program has nominated 66 entry-level and semi-skilled eligible occupations, if the person is working in the Northeast development region. Essentially, a temporary foreign worker, with nine months of full-time employment with an employer, can apply to the PNP program for permanent residency if he or she meets minimum education, English language proficiency, and adequate family income. As noted with the TFWP, the Northeast Pilot Project is important in communities like Dawson Creek where many retail shops and restaurants need to fill entry-level positions that pay minimum wage.

Marketing Basics: A Company Website

In July 2014, the Northern Development Initiative Trust estimated that only 20 per cent of northern businesses had a website.[15] Given that Internet searches are a primary way for many buyers to find supplies and services, it's important to have even a basic online presence. With a well-designed and engaging website, a small firm can appear professional, up-to-date, and possibly larger than it is.

If your firm currently has no website, developing one should be at the top of your marketing "to-do" list. (A good company Facebook page is another alternative, or addition.) Some key pages to include on an effective company site include:

1. **About Us**—This section is likely to be one of the most-visited and a page where prospects head to learn more about your firm. Include content that is fairly brief, to the point, relatable, and—above all— value-focused. "Value-focused" means identifying and explaining the benefits your products and services offer customers. It's much more than a couple of paragraphs on the history of your company.

2. **Services or Products**—Describe clearly the products and/or services your company offers. When a potential client researches companies, this is often the first link that they go to. Think about

including pricing on this page, since it can save the visitor time and leave a good impression. If it is impractical to list pricing, make it easy for a visitor to get in touch by providing a phone number, e-mail address, or a contact form on this page.

3. **Testimonials**—The best way to establish credibility is to provide evidence that your product or service really works. Testimonials from satisfied customers give your product or service credibility. Try to include first, last, and company names, not just a generic, "Bob S." To establish immediate credibility, feature a few of your best testimonials on your homepage.

4. **FAQs**—For some enterprises, it is useful to include a "Frequently Asked Questions" section on the site. This page lists common customer inquiries and provides answers to them. It allows potential customers immediate access to information they might need before buying your product or service.

5. **Contact Information**—To close sales and establish your credibility, provide an e-mail address, telephone number(s), and a mailing address on your site. Make sure these details are clearly visible on every page of the site. Having this information readily accessible makes it easier for customers to reach you. It also helps visitors using mobile devices and enables search engines to properly categorize your page in local search results. You can also set up a contact box that allows customers to get additional information or set up a time to meet. Providing a Google map and written directions can also be useful if you expect regular visitors at your location.

   A word of caution. Businesses that only list email addresses and no other contact details can appear unprofessional and possibly even disreputable.

Some design and usability elements of an effective small business website include:

- **User-friendly navigation**—Nothing will drive visitors away faster than confusing or complicated navigation. Your readers should know where they are on your site at all times, and should easily be able to find pages they've already visited. Each page of your site should have clear links to other important pages or information. Make sure your navigation bar or menu is accessible and easy to understand. It should look exactly the same on every page and always be located in the same place. Avoid long pages of text that force visitors to scroll endlessly (particularly irritating on a mobile device.)

- **Effective sales copy**—The words you use to describe your product and its benefits are critical. Your sales copy may be the only contact you'll have with the vast majority of your visitors. Are the words clear and understandable? Do they invite potential customers to seek more information? Is the content error-free or does it cause the visitor to question the professionalism and trustworthiness of your business?

- Website content should be easy to read with a font of a reasonable size and colour. Format the content for readability by using **line breaks, bullet points, and bolded key words**, so customers can quickly scan for information. If your strengths lie elsewhere, hiring a good copywriter and proofreader will reflect well on your business and enhance its attractiveness to potential clients.

- **Good graphic design and well-chosen images**—A good website designer can help you present your business in a professional yet attractive and appealing manner. Images enable customers to visualize your products or services and their benefits. Be sure to include your company logo and good photos of key products since they can boost your sales. Thoughtful graphic design provides another opportunity to showcase professionalism.

- **Consideration for mobile users**—Mobile browsing and shopping are big trends, so it is vital to have a website that is easy to use with mobile devices. Research conducted for two major U.S. search engines, Google and Bing, showed that between June 2014 and

November 2014 an increasing number of visitors accessed their sites using mobile devices. In June, almost 48 per cent of visitors to Google used mobile devices. By November, mobile users were the majority.[16]

Northern Development Initiative Trust Website

Summary

In short, if you're thinking of starting a business in the North, a lot of useful resources – and people – are available to help. You can do much research even before you travel and make your time in the community as effective as possible. Governments are well aware of the labour shortages that many communities face and are developing programs to try to fill the gap. Money and expertise are there, too. Your time and effort and willingness to reach out can have a big potential impact on the success of your business.

CHAPTER 7

Hit the Ground Running
21.5 Tips from the Locals

> Don't spend so much time trying to choose the perfect
> opportunity that you miss the right opportunity.
>
> Michael Dell

N orthern British Columbia has many well-established businesses and successful entrepreneurs. They're open to new companies coming to their communities (and will put up a solid battle if you're a competitor.) Here's some practical advice people offer, based on their years of northern experience.

1. Get Going!

If you're thinking of establishing a business in the North, the locals' first piece of advice is, "Get going!" With the rush of activity, industrial land is being snapped up quickly. Large, serviced parcels of land are becoming increasingly difficult to find. If multiple LNG plants go ahead, electrical power could become a problem.[1] Surplus, skilled labour is almost non-existent and even unskilled labour is getting harder to find. In Prince Rupert, advertisements for well-paid labouring jobs with full benefits may attract four applicants. In Northeastern communities such as Fort St. John, the price of commercial real estate has doubled between 2012 and 2015.

2. Respect the people

As Dr. Denise Henning, former President of Northwest Community College points out; the people of the North are "hardy, creative, and entrepreneurial people who have to be able to manage boom and bust cycles." Since the 1980s, business people and entire towns, particularly in the Northwest, have had to deal with multiple economic cycles and so have become increasingly self-reliant. As a result, communities in the North have a strong sense of volunteerism and community spirit. Residents are used to taking direct action and take pride in community arenas and civic centres built by locals with funds raised in the community.

Towns and cities in the North survive for economic and social reasons beyond the exploitation of a single resource or because they're next to a major highway. As the authors note in *Investing in Place*: "These communities exist because they have become home to the people who live there, and are, therefore, places worth caring about and working to maintain."[2] To prosper with your business, you will have greater success if you respect community norms and make an effort to fit in.

Keep in mind, as northerners will remind you, much of the wealth of British Columbia comes from resources mined, harvested, and drilled from this region. People are proud of their contribution to the provincial economy and the wealth their businesses create.

3. Talk to local businesses

Ask for 20 minutes of time on the phone, or in person, from a successful, non-competitive business in the community you're targeting. Even in a brief time, it's amazing what you can learn. To be certain of your facts, it's good to check with multiple sources.

Another resource to consider is city hall. Staff usually post the minutes of the city council meetings so you can keep a running tally on the housing starts, number of building permits issued, and other useful commercial information.

4. Prepare your company

If you're planning to supply the multinationals on major projects, either directly or through sub-contracting, consider registering with supply change management auditors like PICS or ISNetworld. Large multinationals use supply chain management services like PICS to pre-qualify and search for vendors. In the words of one Terrace supplier, "You can't just show up on site in some old truck and start working. They'll take one look at you and send you home." You'll need to understand a complex procurement process with companies that have stiff safety and insurance requirements.

Local resources can also get you prepared. For example, the Northern Development Initiative Trust developed a supplier and request for proposal boot camp, to help businesses become part of the local supply chain of goods and services. Camps or other seminars like these can help you get prepared and registered appropriately to be on the preferred local supplier lists of major companies.

5. Build partnerships

In the North, depending on your business, consider two kinds of partnerships to enhance your chances of success. First, explore ways that you might team up with a local firm, either in the same business or one that knows the area well. In the construction sector, many engineering firms will have a good sense of local major projects, timing, and owner needs. A partnership with a company in the same field can help you get work right away and enable you to learn the basics of doing business in the region.

Another key partner could be Aboriginal people. As outlined in Chapter 3, many First Nations in the North have established economic development corporations that are signing joint-venture and other agreements with companies large and small. By working in partnership, you gain access to workers who will stay in the region, local knowledge, and can tap into a young, growing consumer market. Local retail and restaurant owners who hire Aboriginal employees meet staffing needs and also reap the marketing benefits of having workers that mirror a large part of their customer base.

6. Visit, learn, and look around before you invest

It's important to spend some time in the North exploring your business options, before committing. As one businessman said to me, "There's a benefit of visiting the area to see up close what is happening and speaking to as many people as possible."

Case Study: Real estate development

David McIntosh (not his real name) is a Vancouver businessman who worked for many years in Hong Kong and the Asia-Pacific region. He returned to Canada and in 2013 began looking for investment opportunities. He'd heard a lot was going on in Northern BC, so made several visits to Kitimat in the Northwest and then Fort St. John in the Northeast. In Fort St. John, he met with the local economic development office, city planner, local chamber of commerce, real estate agents, bankers, business people, and others. He returned a second time a few months later for a follow-up visit.

After exploring various options, including retail opportunities, David decided to look more closely at residential real estate. He and his partner have built up a portfolio of new units geared to providing temporary housing to the managers of major firms involved with Site C and LNG development. David worked with a regional developer whom he met after an introduction from another economic development office. This developer had great success with the same sort of project in another northern town. The units have sold out and McIntosh is now looking at other opportunities in the North.

You also can learn a lot by attending local conferences. For example, every year in January, Prince George hosts the Premier's National Resources Forum, with various speakers for key resource sectors. Prior to the Forum, Initiatives Prince George, an economic development agency, holds a one day workshop with eight to 10 major companies presenting on the procurement needs and processes. In the Northwest, Prince Rupert hosts the Northwest Growth Conference. It provides another occasion to learn about procurement options as a result of major project activity in that region. Webinars of various topics are also frequently available.

7. Make use of local/regional business resources

Towns in the North generally have active and engaged local and regional economic development offices. (At one point in a northwest town, some large local companies even funded a private consultant to lead their efforts to develop the area.) With the growth in the region, they've become much more active and can be a good source of leads or provide a good overview of economic activities. Chambers of Commerce can also be helpful and often put on useful lunches or meetings. The Fort St. John Chamber organized business matching days for suppliers interested in BC Hydro's Site C dam project; on another occasion it brought in a major pipeline developer to outline the company's plans and supplier needs. (See Chapter 1 and the Appendices for more information on local business resources.)

8. Find a niche and fill it

Think about a business that offers services that are unavailable in the North or are hard to find, then fill that niche. One local restaurant owner told me the story of the "grease cleaner guys." Canadian fire codes require that all restaurants have their kitchen hood and vents inspected and cleaned professionally, some parts monthly, quarterly, or once a year. Two "local guys" started a firm to deal with this messy job that few like to tackle. These entrepreneurs put up a one page website, advertised, and soon had a quasi-monopoly on the service, charging $600 per clean, doing four restaurants per day. They are now busily expanding to service other northern towns and mine sites, along with the increasing numbers of remote camps being established throughout the region.

Professional services, specialty retail, restaurants (in 2015, one of the few Indian restaurants in the Dawson Creek area closed when the owner retired), and many other businesses are in demand. In some towns, shortages can be acute for basic business services such as bookkeeping; suppliers with minimal training were commanding premium prices. Yoga instructor? In some communities you may be run off your feet with clients!

9. Consider buying an existing business

Between 2015 and 2019, over 25 per cent of companies in BC will be up for sale. Many successful business owners in northern towns are near retirement age and are looking to sell. (In fact, some even retire early: there are quite a few young retirees in the North, with significant funds.) Sometimes they end up closing instead, for want of buyers, even though the business is profitable with a good customer base. If you prefer to buy an existing operation, think about contacting a local accounting firm or the town's economic development office for possibilities.

Takeovers or mergers could be another possibility. In Terrace in 2013, Stantec, a North American environmental consulting firm, took over locally-owned, 25-person Cambria Gordon. The larger company established a local presence in a region with numerous major projects requiring environmental work; the smaller firm was able to work on these big jobs.

10. Leave the suit at home

Professional dress in the North is more relaxed than in major cities. Wearing a suit and fancy shoes immediately dubs you as an outsider. You also have to be practical; in some towns, the sidewalks, despite the best efforts of local authorities, are covered in gravel and grit. I have my "northern shoes" that I wear when I'm travelling—they're solid, sensible, and made of strong leather. Think functional business-casual for most meetings and you'll be fine.

11. Build a local presence

If you're planning to establish a long term presence, get involved in community activities. Attend local Chamber of Commerce events, such as business excellence awards or trade shows. Join the Rotary or another service club and help out with fundraising and other charitable activities. The business community in the North is small; your presence or absence in supporting it will be noted. Making the effort can pay off in other ways, too—the connections and advice you can get through participation can be invaluable.

Advice from Northern Development

Northern Development Initiative Trust (www.northerndevelopment.bc.ca), is an independent, regionally operated, economic development funding corporation for Central and Northern BC. It provides funding for projects that support economic development and regional diversification. Here's some advice for entrepreneurs from Joel McKay, Director of Communications.

1. **Get here**—Don't think you can do business in Northern BC without first spending time in Northern BC.

2. **Know your geography**—Northern BC is the size of France and each area is unique and diverse. Learn about the mountain ranges, the watersheds, the First Nations, and communities: all of these things play an integral role in feasibility and decision making associated with major projects and investments.

3. **Relationships are everything**—Business in this region is largely done based on existing relationships and word-of-mouth. Your reputation is everything – take time to get to know people and listen to their goals.

4. **Seek out investment opportunities**—There are many long-standing small and medium enterprises without succession plans. Find them! These could be first-rate investment opportunities.

5. **Don't overlook funding opportunities**—There are dozens of foundations, trusts, and funding agencies throughout Northern BC that support big projects, small projects, and a variety of businesses and industries. Connect with them! You could qualify for funding.

Tip: Northern Development, as the region's only economic development trust and largest granting organization, is a good place to start when looking for funding opportunities.

12. Be accurate. Be fearless.

In the words of one economic development leader; "Do your homework, ask around, and make sure you've got accurate information about the market opportunity for your business—then don't look back. Take the plunge and start. Be nimble and adjust to changing circumstances, but most of all, be fearless."

13. Take advantage of funding opportunities

Are you contemplating setting up a tech company? Have you considered the North? Often provincial or federal funding or regional grants are available for these and other types of businesses. Sometimes you'll have minimal competition for some useful dollars when you're just getting started.

14. Make the North your base

The North has a myriad of business opportunities available. Young business people or professionals can work on projects or assignments that ramp up their experience far faster than in large cities. You may find plenty of business locally and keep your focus there. Alternatively, if you do good work for multinational firms on major projects in the North, you may find your business gets ongoing contracts in other parts of Canada and the world.

15. Market to Aboriginal people directly

If you are in the retail or hospitality sector, consider marketing directly to Aboriginal people. Your business can advertise directly, through such means as the CFNR network, First Nations Radio, that is broadcast to over 50 communities in Northern BC. You can sponsor sports events (the All Native Basketball Tournament in Prince Rupert attracts over 50 teams), celebrations (HOBIYEE is the Nisga'a Nation's celebration of the February Moon), donate prizes to community fund-raising events, and so forth. Of course, one of the best means of attracting clientele is to have your staff mirror the community.

16. Never underestimate the weather

Global warming or not, it can get cold in the North, particularly in the Northeast. Storms, fog, ice, and snow can wreak havoc with the supply chain or your travel plans. Even the locals may slide off the road with the first snowfall. Leave yourself some slack when making schedules that involve moving people and/or goods over long distances.

17. Be creative about staffing

Staffing in the North can be a challenge, as outlined in Chapter 6. You'll likely have to be creative and consider hiring employees from non-traditional pools. Many communities have multicultural or diversity societies that are often the first place newcomers to Canada stop when they move north. Though the rules are tightening, you may need to think about hiring Temporary Foreign Workers—either directly from abroad, or from major cities like Vancouver. In 2015, Canada started a new immigration system, whereby you can hire Express Entry candidates to meet your labour needs when you are unable to find Canadians or permanent residents to fill job vacancies. In addition, the federal government will introduce a matching function to connect eligible employers with Express Entry candidates. The BC government also has the Provincial Nominee Program which can be an attractive recruitment option. Don't forget family; one economic development officer told me about a father, son, and cousins that came to her community to develop a new subdivision, with other family members and friends providing additional labour.

HOW TO...

ENGAGE AND RETAIN MILLENNIALS

Provide coaching. Offer them an opportunity to explore different roles within the company.

Let them practice being entrepreneurs by funding projects to complete internally.

Avoid burning out your high performers.

Foster a company culture that encourages people to care about each other and their work.

Be clear and open about the career paths available within the company.

Photo: Michael Ford Photography

18. Be prepared for pent up demand

If you're bringing a new service to a northern town or opening up a well-known franchise, be prepared to deal with the happy challenge of pent-up demand. The opening of a well-known coffee and donut franchise like Tim Horton's can be front page news in the local paper. Sporting goods retailers also have seen huge lines on opening days. People in the North often have limited local shopping options; if you're expanding the availability of local goods or entertainment and filling a niche, you'll be welcomed. (Currently, many restaurant chains do some of their best business in Canada in Northeast BC.) The same holds true for professional service or private health care providers; if few are available locally, you'll have a lot of business when you open up.

19. Infrastructure matters

Weather and remoteness can make for limited accessibility in some places. In the Northeast, for example, industry has complained for years that in the Pine Pass on Highway 97, the existing height and width constraints of railway passes and bridges hamper their ability to diversify manufacturing. These infrastructure constraints also make it hard to supply and move large equipment and loads to and from Northeast BC and the rest of the province. Depending on your location, cell phone coverage can be spotty as you travel through the region. Large airlines have started to serve smaller communities, bringing a welcome drop in prices for air travel, but flights, particularly on weekends, can be limited. These problems will be addressed over time, but until they are, you need to think about your business needs and any issues that weaknesses in infrastructure might create.

20. Plan for the down times

Prices for commodities follow a boom and bust cycle and can greatly affect some local economies. Certainly, with long term contracts for resources and the establishment of more government services in the region, the "bust" times in the North may be less daunting than in the past. If you're thinking of setting up a long-term business, when you plan, you need to take the cyclical nature of many industries into account.

21. Embrace the northern lifestyle

Each northern community offers a unique rhythm and lifestyle. What they have in common is close proximity to nature, friendly people, and ample opportunities to become active and engaged in civic life. Becoming part of the local scene is much easier than in a large city. There are a myriad of festivals and fairs year round and towns have a more active cultural life than you might expect, given their size. More immigrants and young people from larger urban centres are making their way north, joining those who settled there in the 1950s and 1960s. It is a different way of life, but if you embrace it, the North can be a great place to live. As many locals say, they came to a town "to make money for a few years" but then never left. If you find that you like the North, the same may be true for you and your family. (See Chapter 5 for more details.)

Supply Chain Connector

The Supply Chain Connector (www.supplychainconnector.ca) is a free database that includes 2,100 businesses based in central and northern BC. Designed by Northern Development, it was launched in 2013. This resource is designed specifically to get industrial supply chain businesses in front of procurement officers for major projects, hopefully resulting in more contracts awarded to northern-based businesses.

21.5 Be adventurous and have fun!

Look upon doing business in the North with a sense of adventure. There are opportunities galore to do good business, if you're willing to take some risks and engage in the new. Go for it!

Conclusion

After you have read all the chapters in *British Columbia's New North*, you should have a good grasp of the opportunities the North offers and the steps you need to take to get your business launched there. But you need to put these ideas and recommendations into action. It will be hard to remember everything—so keep the book handy, and review the sections that apply to your business or current concerns at any given time. Taking this step will have a positive impact on your business in the future.

For example, if you are meeting with an Aboriginal economic development corporation for the first time, check out Chapters 2 and 3 on Aboriginal Peoples to help you prepare. Wondering about staffing issues? Chapter 6, "A Business Roadmap," has some ideas for different labour pools you might want to explore. Or if you are considering commercial possibilities, have a look at Chapter 4, "A Dynamic Decade," for a great review of some major projects and opportunities in northern communities. You get the drift—this book covers a lot of ground and is chock a block with good information. If you have suggestions on ways we can improve the next edition, please let us know at newnorth @ ingenia-consulting.com.

I tell the participants at the end of my seminars that they have been given knowledge, tools, and resources to more effectively start or expand a business in Northern British Columbia—if they choose to do so. And I wish them well on that journey.

I wish you the same success. See you up North!

Acknowledgements

To say this book is "by Ramona Materi" overstates the case, since without significant help from other people, it would have only remained an idea.

To start, I would like to thank members of the research team, including Eugene Chu, Morgan Hordal, Nicole Morrison, Carmen Reems, and Alec Robson. As a consultant and economist I deal with the present and future. Their digging around in the stacks and databases of university libraries and in the far corners of the Internet helped me to gain a better understanding of the rich history and traditions of the North, its industries, its communities, and its people.

Thank you and a tip of the hat to my editor, Lorn Kennedy, whose eagle eye and knowledge of the North made each chapter better. Kudos, too, to our design team of Madelyn Hambly, Stéphane Gibelin, and Iryna Spica.

We were fortunate to have the participation of many people, in the North and elsewhere, who patiently answered our questions in interviews, and verified facts and our conclusions. To each of the following individuals, I hope this book captures the best of what you told us.

Lori Ackerman, Anna Barley, Ron Bartlett, Jeff Beale, Tiffany Bell, Paul Bjorn, Adam Clark, Frank Cook, David Conway, Brian Downey, Natalie Dupont, Rob Dykman, Art Erasmus, Oksana Exell, Mani Fallon, Kerry France, Kiel Giddens, Moira Green, Greg Halseth, David Hanley, Lilia Hansen, Shauna Harper, Daria Hasselmann, Dr. Denise Henning, David Hoff, Art Jarvis, Jeannette Karasiuk, Melanie Karjala, John Kason, Dale Lamoureux, Baila Lazarus, Anastasia Lewdon, Wilfred Major, Janet Marren, Gerry Martin, Lael McKeown, Chris McLean, Blair Moffat, Kelley Moffat, Blaine Moore, Theresa Mucci-Rodgers, Rick Newlove, Trang Nguyen, Heather Oland, Andrea Palmer, Maria Pavao, Anthony Perl, Vince Prince, Laurie Rancourt,

Team members Jenna Materi and Melanie Robson

Ray, Ron Rodgers, Charles Scott, Susan Stearn, George Weinand, Stuart and Marie Wilmot, Scott Wisdahl, and Don Zurowski.

I would like to thank also the Economic Development Officers and Chamber of Commerce staff who helped us to fact-check and enhance the economic snapshots of major communities in the North. They include Jaylene Arnold, Christina Doll, Moira Green, Sue Kenny, Blaine Moore, Trish Parsons, Amber Sheasgreen, Allan Stroet, and Paul Vendittelli. Hats off, as well, to everyone at Initiatives Prince George and Northern Development Initiative Trust for all their help.

The pull-boxes and quotations in this book add immensely valuable information for readers. For their expertise and willingness to contribute, I am grateful to Laurie Dolan, Moira Green, Bob Joseph, Joel McKay, Alex Pietralla, Catherine Sas, Baljit Sethi, Murray Slezak, Sandra Sutter, and Cherie Williams. Also, thank you to Roy Millen and the Canadian Federation of Independent Business for allowing us to quote from their articles. And thanks to Initiatives Prince George and Kismenio Somcio for providing photos and Business in Vancouver/EcoTrust and BC Hydro for their map and image.

I am particularly indebted to a large number of critical readers who read drafts of the manuscript and offered useful and enlightening comments and suggestions for improvement. Their ideas and perspectives continually reinforced my faith in the potential of the project. For their frankness and insights, I would like to thank:

Colleen Annibal, Jaylene Arnold, Kathy Bedard, Tiffany Bell, Sandra Berman, Ralph Bullis, Adam Clark, Paul Crosby, Bob Davidson, Laurie Dolan, Michael Donelson, Seth Downs, David Dunlop, Dr. Pat Fahy, Scott Harrison, Pat Hufnagel-Smith, Jill and Gary Ley, Sherry Little, Kelly Louie, Jenna Materi, Gerry MacDonald, Joel McKay, Lael McKeown, Barry and Eunice Nicolle, Maria Pavao, Kate Pelletier, Miranda Post, Vince Prince, Sasha Ramnarine, Sonia Ribaux, Hannah Robson, Murray Slezak, Christina Solf, Melissa Sonberg, Sandra Sutter, Sarah Louise Turner, Cherie Williams, and Scott Wisdahl.

And of course, I extend my sincere appreciation to Dr. Charles Jago for writing the foreword to this book and to Mayor Dale Bumstead, Shauna Harper, Mark Hoag, Ron Poole, and Shauna Wouters for providing testimonials.

I would like to make particular note of the support, advice, and encouragement I received from Dr. Pat Fahy, Jill and Gary Ley, Lael McKeown, Kate Pelletier, Sasha Ramnarine, and Murray Slezak. Writing a book can be a long process and I truly appreciated their ongoing interest in the project.

Finally, I extend an extra special thank you to Melanie Robson, who managed the many "bits and pieces" that make up this book, ably contacted and coordinated a multitude of people, and devoted many hours to bringing it all together.

Ramona Materi
Written within the traditional territories of
the Musqueam, Squamish and Tsleil-Waututh Nations
Vancouver, British Columbia

Appendices

APPENDIX 1
Economic Development Organizations in Northern BC
(Contacts current as of June 2015)

Community Organizations

Northern Development Initiative Trust
www.northerndevelopment.bc.ca
301 – 1268 Fifth Avenue
Prince George, BC V2L 3L2
info@northerndevelopment.bc.ca
250-561-2525

Northwest/Central

District of Kitimat
Economic Development
www.kitimat.ca
272 City Centre, Kitimat, BC V8C 2H7
Rose Klukas
Director of Economic Development
250-632-8921

Prince George
Initiatives Prince George Economic
Development
www.initiativespg.com
Suite 201 – 1300 First Avenue
Prince George, BC V2L 2Y3
info@initiativespg.com
250-649-3200

Prince Rupert
Prince Rupert and Port Edward
Economic Development Corporation
www.predc.com
424 - 3rd Avenue West
Prince Rupert, BC V8J 1L7
Paul Vendittelli
Economic Development Officer
paul.vendittelli@princerupert.ca
250-627-5138

Smithers
Bulkley Valley Economic
Development Association
(Smithers and Wet'suwet'en First
Nation and the Regional District of
Bulkley Nechako Area 'A')
bveda.ca
201 - 3848 3rd Ave., Smithers
Box 3243 Smithers, BC V0J 2N0
Allan Stroet
allanstroet@bveda.ca
250-847-4355

Terrace
Terrace Economic Development
www.teda.ca
3224 Kalum Street
Terrace, BC V8G 2N1
250-635-4168, 1-877-635-4168

District of Vanderhoof
Economic Development
www.vanderhoof.ca
160 Connaught Street, P.O. Box 900
Vanderhoof, BC V0J 3A0
edo@district.vanderhoof.ca
250-567-4711

Northeast

Chetwynd Economic Development
www.gochetwynd.com
5400 North Access Road, Box 357
Chetwynd, BC V0C 1J0
Economic Development Officer
Ellen McAvany
calliou@gochetwynd.com
250-401-4113

Community Futures Peace Liard
communityfutures.biz
904 - 102nd Ave
Dawson Creek BC V1G 2B7
Economic Development Coordinator
Sue Kenny
skenny@communityfutures.biz
250-782-8748, 1-877-296-5888

Dawson Creek
www.dawsoncreek.ca/business
Box 150, Dawson Creek, BC V1G 4G4
10105 - 12A Street
Dawson Creek, BC V1G 3V7
admin@dawsoncreek.ca
250-784-3600

Fort Nelson
Community Development and
Planning Department
www.northernrockies.ca
5319 - 50th Avenue South
Bag Service 399
Fort Nelson, BC V0C 1R0
ecdev@northernrockies.ca
250-774-2541 (2045)

Fort St. John
Economic Development
www.fortstjohn.ca
10631 - 100 Street
Fort St. John, BC V1J 3Z5
economicdevelopment@fortstjohn.ca
250-787-5787

North Peace Economic Development Commission
npedc.ca
9505 100th St.
Fort St. John, BC V1J 4N4
invest@npedc.ca
250-785-5969

South Peace Economic Development Commission
www.southpeacebc.ca
Box 810, 1981 Alaska Avenue
Dawson Creek, BC V1G 4H8
info@southpeacebc.ca
250-784-3200, 1-800-670-7773

Tumbler Ridge
Economic Development
www.investtumblerridge.ca
Economic Development Officer
Jordan Wall
edo@dtr.ca
250-242-4242

Aboriginal Economic Development Organizations

Northwest/Central

Haida Nations

HaiCo Foundation for Economic
Development
www.haico.ca
PO Box 1384, Unit 1, Commercial
Centre, Skidegate, BC V0T 1S1
info@haico.ca
250-559-6809

Haisla First Nations

haisla.ca
HNC Administration Office
500 Gitksan Ave., Haisla PO Box 1101
Kitamaat Village BC V0T 2B0
Jason Majore, Chief Operating Officer
250-639-9361 (122)

Kitselas

Kitselas Development Corporation
www.kitselas.com
4562 Queensway Unit: K
Terrace, BC V8G 3X6
j.dopson@kitselasdlp.ca
250-638-8881

Kitsumkalum

Economic Development
www.kitsumkalum.bc.ca/business.html
P.O. Box 544, Terrace, BC V8G 4B5
3514 West Kalum Road
Terrace, BC V8G 0C8
kitsumkalum@citywest.ca
250-635-5000 local 102

Lax Kw'alaams Band

laxkwalaams.ca
206 Shashaak Street
Lax Kw'alaams, BC V0V 1H0
Economic Development Officer
Bob Maraes
Bob.ecdev.laxband@gmail.com
250-625-3293

Lheidli T'enneh First Nation

Economic Development
www.lheidli.ca
1041 Whenun Road
Prince George, BC V2K 5X8
info@lheidli.ca
250-963-8451, 1-877-963-8451

Metlakatla First Nation

Metlakatla Development Corporation
www.metlakatla.ca
P.O. Box 224
Prince Rupert, BC V8J 3P6
Harold Leighton, CEO
hleighton@metlakatla.ca
250-628-3201

Morricetown First Nation

Economic Development
www.moricetown.ca
Suite 3 - 205 Beaver Road
Smithers, BC V0J 2N1
ecdev@moricetown.ca
250-847-2133

Nadleh Whut'En First Nation

www.nadleh.ca
P.O. Box 36, Fort Fraser, BC V0J 1N0
Chief Martin Louie
4dakelh@nadleh.ca
250-690-7211

Nak'azdli First Nation

www.nakazdli.ca
Nak'azdli Band Office, P.O. Box 1329
284 Kwah Road
Fort St. James, BC V0J 1P0
Economic Development Officer
leonardt@nakazdli.ca
250-996-7171

Nee Tahi Buhn Band

47805 Olson Road
Burns Lake, BC V0J 1E4
R.R.#2, Site 7, Comp 28
Burns Lake, BC V0J 1E0
Chief Raymond Morris
generalmanager@ntbband.ca
250-694-3494

Nisga'a Nation

Economic Development Department
www.nisgaanation.ca
Bert Mercer
Economic Development Manager
Nisga'a Lisims Government
P.O. Box 231, 2000 Lisims Drive
Gitlaxt'aamiks Village Government,
BC V0J 1A0
bertramm@nisgaa.net
250-633 3000, 1-866-633-0888

Saik'uz First Nation

Natural Resource Department
www.saikuz.com
Saik'uz First Nation Band Office
135 Joseph Street
Vanderhoof, BC V0J 3A1
Lands & Resource Manager
jackie.thomas@saikuz.com
250-567-9293

Skin Tyee First Nation

Box 131, Southbank, BC V0J 2P0
Chief Rene Skin
admin@skintyeenation.ca
250-694-3517

Stellat'en First Nation

www.stellaten.ca
Stella Road P.O. Box 760
Fraser Lake, BC V0J 1S0
Chief Archie Patrick
chiefpatrick@stellatenfirstnation.ca
250-699-8747

Tahltan Central Council

Tahltan Nation Development
Corporation (TNDC)
www.tndc.ca
P.O. Box 250 Dease Lake, BC V0C 1L0
250-771-5482, 1-866-827-8632

Takla Lake Band

www.taklafn.ca
Land and Economics
Takla Landing BC V0J 2TO
Councillor John A. French
250-996-7877, 1-877-794-7877

Ts'il Kaz Koh
www.burnslakeband.ca
Burns Lake Band
675 Hwy 16 W, Burns Lake
Bag 9000, Burns Lake, BC V0J 1E0
Chief Wesley Sam
250-692-7717

Wet'suwet'en First Nation
Yinka Dene Economic Development
Limited Partnership
www.ydedlp.com
P.O. Box 245, Burns Lake, BC V0J 1E0
ydedlp@ydedlp.com
250-698-7770

Northeast

Fort Nelson First Nation
Economic Development
www.fortnelsonfirstnation.org
RR1 Mile 295 Alaska Highway
Fort Nelson, BC V0C 1R0
250-774-7257, 1-888-543-3636

McLeod Lake Indian Band
Tse'khene Community Development
Corporation
www.mlib.ca/tsekhene-community-
development-corporation
61 Sekani Drive
McLeod Lake, BC V0J2G0
Economic Development Officer
Lucy Martin
250-750-4415, 1-888-822-1143

Treaty 8 Tribal Association
(Includes Doig River, Halfway River,
Prophet River, Saulteau, West Moberly,
Blueberry River, Fort Nelson, McLeod
Lake)
Kihew-Sas Ventures Ltd.
treaty8.bc.ca
10233 100th Avenue
Fort St. John, BC V1J 1Y8
250-785-0612, ext. 225

West Moberly First Nations
Dunne-za Ventures LP
www.dunneza.com
9203-109 Street
Fort St. John, BC V1J 6K6
william@dunneza.com
1-877-787-5084

BC Métis Federation
bcmetis.com
Head Office: 300 – 3665 Kingsway
Vancouver, BC V5R 5W2
Info@BCMetis.com
604-638-7220

Métis Nation BC
www.mnbc.ca
30691 Simpson Road
Abbotsford, BC V2T 6C7
Ministry of Economic Development
Minister Glen Ohs, gohs@mnbc.ca
604-557-5851, 1-800-940-1150

Appendix 2

Sample Competency Job Description

Job: Construction Worker

Job Summary: Physical labour at building, highway, and heavy construction projects, tunnel and shaft excavations, and demolition sites.

Responsibilities

- Dig, spread, and level dirt and gravel, using pick and shovel
- Lift, carry, and hold building materials, tools, and supplies
- Clean tools, equipment, materials, and work areas
- Mix, pour, and spread concrete, asphalt, gravel, and other materials, using hand tools
- Operate hand and power tools of all types: air hammers, earth tampers, cement mixers, small mechanical hoists, surveying and measuring equipment, and a variety of other equipment and instruments

Education and Credentials

Proof of Occupational First Aid Level 1 or Equivalent as acceptable to WorkSafe BC.

General Competencies

Competency	Description
Concern for Safety	Identifies hazardous or potentially hazardous situations and takes appropriate action to maintain a safe environment for self and others
Resilience	Remains energized and focused in the face of ambiguity, change or strenuous demands
Quality Focus	Follows up procedures, ensures high quality output, takes action to solve quality problems or notify quality issues as appropriate
Planning and Organizing	Developing, implementing, evaluating, and adjusting plans to reach goals, while ensuring the optimal use of resources.
Teamwork	Working collaboratively with others to achieve organizational goals
Attention to Detail	Working in a conscientious, consistent, and thorough manner

APPENDIX 3
Sample Competency Based Interview Questions

Job: Construction Worker

General Competencies

Competency	Interview Questions
Concern for Safety	**Questions to ask** 1. What were the major safety requirements of your previous job? Did these requirements sometimes interfere with your work? How did you handle it? 2. Please tell me about a time when you saw something happening that was potentially unsafe? What was the situation? What rules/procedures were involved? What did you do? What happened? 3. Have you had an accident or a close call? What happened? What did you do? **What to listen for in answers** • Follows health and safety guidelines • Understands and applies health and safety regulations and policies that relate to own position • Maintains/updates own knowledge of safety issues • Acts to correct obviously unsafe conditions in the work place • Informs appropriate person and documents incident according to workplace procedures

Photo: Progressive Ventures Construction

Terrace, British Columbia

Competency	Interview Questions
Resilience	**Questions to ask** 1. Describe a situation in which you suffered a major disappointment. How did you deal with it? 2. Tell me about a situation where you were asked to do something you didn't think you could do. How did you handle it? 3. What were the worst working conditions you ever experienced? How did you handle them?
	What to listen for in answers • Works effectively in the face of occasional strenuous work demands • Remains effective and retains perspective in the face of periodic disruptions (e.g., identifies own personal limit for work load and makes appropriate adjustments) • While remaining open to other viewpoints, demonstrates realistic confidence in own abilities, views or decisions when challenged • Demonstrates an awareness of how own actions or reactions impact others (i.e., others' stress levels) and adjusts behaviour accordingly • Takes steps to deal constructively with setbacks
Planning and Organizing	**Questions to ask** 1. Tell me about a time when your schedule was upset by something unplanned. What did you do? 2. How do you decide which activities have top priorities on your time?
	What to listen for in answers • Plans and organizes own activities to accomplish pre-determined standards or procedures • Asks questions on priorities as needed • Monitors the quality and timeliness of own work • Responsibly uses the resources at one's immediate disposal

Competency	Interview Questions
Teamwork	**Questions to ask**
	1. Tell me about a situation where you had to work with other people to get something done. How did you decide who did what? What happened?
	2. Have you ever had a situation where someone you worked with didn't finish their task, which meant you couldn't do yours? What did you do? What happened?
	What to listen for in answers
	• Deals honestly and fairly with others, showing consideration and respect for individual differences
	• Does own fair share of the work
	• Seeks assistance from other team members, as needed
	• Helps other team members
	• Shares all relevant information with others
Attention to Detail	**Questions to ask**
	1. Have you ever had an experience in which you were glad you had paid attention to some particular detail? Please describe it.
	2. Have you ever found an error in your own work? How did it happen? What did you do about it?
	What to listen for in answers
	• Recognizes less obvious information
	• Verifies assumptions and information before accepting them
	• Seeks out others to check or review own work
	• Reviews all relevant information or aspects of a situation before taking action or making a decision

Notes

Chapter 1

1. BC Stats 2013, Statistics Canada 2013.
2. BC Stats 2013.
3. Government of British Columbia, "Natural Gas" Retrieved from http://www.britishcolumbia.ca/invest/industry-sectors/natural-gas.aspx#.VWs_Lc9VhHw.
4. Mining Association of BC. Retrieved from www.mining.bc.ca
5. Association for Mineral Exploration British Columbia, www.amebc.ca
6. Don Krusel, The Vancouver Sun, "Opinion: Diversification driving growth at Port of Prince Rupert," February 10, 2015.

Chapter 2

1. George Hammond, "Study undermines narrative of B.C. First Nations as simple hunter-gatherers," *Vancouver Sun*, April 11, 2015.
2. Terminology, particularly as it relates to First Peoples, can be confusing—because it is! Various Nations identify themselves in different ways: for example, there are groups such as the Haisla First Nation and the McLeod Lake Indian Band. Because of these differences, many people do not feel confident using certain terms when referring to Aboriginal Peoples. If you're not sure of what term to use, ask the group you're dealing with for their preference. In this book, I use the terms that business organizations in British Columbia typically employ in 2015– Aboriginal Peoples, referring to the three groups as defined in the Canadian Constitution, which are made up of First Nations (rather than the term "Indians" that the Constitution uses), the Inuit, and the Métis. In cases where I quote other speakers or documents, I have kept the terminology that they used.
3. "Report of Royal Commission on Aboriginal Peoples: Restructuring the Relationship, Part One, Volume 2," *Royal Commission on Aboriginal Peoples*, 1996.
4. Treaty 8 is one of eleven numbered treaties made between the Government of Canada and First Nations. It was signed in 1899 and covers First Nations in BC and Alberta.
5. See Olive Patricia Dickason, *A Concise History of Canada's First Nations*, 2nd ed (Don Mills, Ont.; New York: Oxford University Press, 2010).

6. Dana Lepofsky et al., "Ancient Shellfish Mariculture on the Northwest Coast of North America," *American Antiquity* 80, no. 2 (April 1, 2015): 236–59.

7. See Jesse Morin, "The Political Economy of Stone Celt Exchange in Pre-Contact British Columbia: The Salish Nephrite/jade Industry" 2012.

8. See Helen Meilleur, *A Pour of Rain: Stories from a West Coast Fort* (Vancouver, B.C: Raincoast Books, 2001).

9. J. Gosnell, "Official Report of Debates of the Legislative Assembly," December 2, 1998.

10. Ibid.

11. Some may question my use of the phrase "largely negative." As noted in the Interim Report of the Canadian Truth and Reconciliation Commission 2012, p. 7, "Many former students also expressed gratitude for the education they received, and spoke of the long-lasting relations that had developed between some teachers and students, and especially among the students themselves, who became family away from home. The Commission also heard about the fun that children had in school. In the presence of a dedicated teacher, some children experienced the pleasure of learning. While traditional Aboriginal games were undermined, many told of how they survived through their participation in sports or the arts. In some cases, particularly in more recent years, parents had sent them to school to learn the skills needed to make a contribution on behalf of their people. The Commission heard about how these students made, and are continuing to make, those contributions." Retrieved April 26, 2015 from www.myrobust.com/websites/trcinstitution/File/Interim%20report%20English%20electronic.pdf.

12. Gilbert Oskaboose, "Letting Go of Residential Schools," November 1993, Retrieved January 5, 2015 from firstperspective.ca.

13. "Royal Commission on Aboriginal Peoples, Final Report." Indian and Northern Affairs Canada, February 8, 2006.

14. "Aboriginals Sue Canadian Government over Adoptions to White Families during 1960s." *The Canadian Press*, February 10, 2015.

15. Aboriginal Affairs and Northern Development Canada. "Prime Minister Harper offers full apology on behalf of Canadians for the Indian Residential Schools system," September 9, 2010 www.aadnc-aandc.gc.ca/eng/1100100015644/1100100015649 (January 5, 2015).

16. Royal Canadian Mounted Police Government of Canada, "Missing and Murdered Aboriginal Women: A National Operational Overview," May 27, 2014, http://www.rcmp-grc.gc.ca/pubs/mmaw-faapd-eng.htm.

17. Nationtalk, "Treaty 8 First Nations Head to Court to Fight for Their Treaty Rights," Nation Talk, April 23, 2015 http://nationtalk.ca/story/treaty-8-first-nations-head-to-court-to-fight-for-their-treaty-rights.

18. Doug Eyford, "Eyford Report," December 5, 2013 (April 2015).

19. Irene Lanzinger and Niels Veldhuis. "Head to Head: What Should the B.C. Government's Top 2015 Economic Priorities Be?" Business in Vancouver, January 20, 2015.

20. "Affirmation of the Nemiah Declaration, March 19, 2015." http://www.tsilhqotin.ca/PDFs/Nemiah_Declaration.pdf.

21. Eyford, p. 59.

Chapter 3

1. Chief Clarence Louie, Speaking Notes, First Nations Economic Forum. November 7-9, 2005, Calgary, Alberta.

2. See Derek Burleton and Sonya Gulati, "Estimating the Size of the Aboriginal Market in Canada," Special Report TD Economics (TD Economics, June 17, 2011).

3. See Derek Burleton and Sonya Gulati, "Estimating the Size of the Aboriginal Market in Canada," Special Report TD Economics (TD Economics, June 17, 2011).

4. Peter O'Neil, "First Nations Inc: Entrepreneurs take over, Some First Nations look to business rather than the courts for solutions," *Vancouver Sun*, September 18, 2014.

5. See Bryan Gallagher and Thomas B. Lawrence, "Entrepreneurship and Indigenous Identity: A Study of Identity Work by Indigenous Entrepreneurs in British Columbia," *International Journal of Entrepreneurship and Small Business* 17, no. 4 (2012): 395.

6. Barbara Shecter, "An 'emerging market' at home: Canada's banks making a big push into aboriginal communities," *Financial Post*, January 10, 2015.

7. Tom Gierasimczuk, "New Travel Agency Launched by Aboriginal Tourism BC. BC Business," April 28 2014 www.bcbusiness.ca/tourism-culture/new-travel-agency-launched-by-aboriginal-tourism-bc (March 15 2015).

8. "Aboriginal Participation in Trades and Apprenticeship in B.C," ITA, August 27, 2012.

9. Annie Turner et al., *Aboriginal Peoples in Canada - First Nations People, Métis and Inuit National Household Survey, 2011.* [Ottawa, Ont.]: Statistics Canada, 2013. http://www.deslibris.ca/ID/237902.

Chapter 4

1. Stephen Hume, "B.C's North: The Mystique and the Reality," *Vancouver Sun*, September 6, 2013.

2. Presentation by Renata King, Northern Development Initiatives Trust, January 2015, to Initiatives Prince George Marketing Forum.

3. Shawn McCarthy, "Canada's LNG Marathon Man: Pioneering the Dream from Coast to Coast," *The Globe and Mail*, February 27, 2015.

4. BC LNG Alliance, "Moving Natural Gas Safely Across BC," A special series on Liquefied Natural Gas, *North Shore News*, May 3, 2015.

5. Honourable Christie Clark, responding to questions from Liberal Party members, May 14, 2015.

6. BC Hydro Fact Sheet. Planning, Evaluation and Development, Retrieved from http://bchydro.com.

7. Alan Taylor, "The Exxon Valdez Oil Spill: 25 Years Ago Today," *The Atlantic*, March 24, 2014, sec. In Focus.

8. Gordon Hoekstra, "Northern B.C. Companies Want a Piece of Billions of Dollars in Energy Projects, *Vancouver Sun*, July 3, 2014.

9. Interview with Rick Newlove, Manager, Enform, Fort St. John, April 10, 2015.

Chapter 5

1. Frank O'Brien, "Housing in the North," *Business in Vancouver*, February 9, 2015

2. "British Columbia's Housing Cost Comparison," Northern Development, March 5, 2014.

3. "Smithers Community Profile," Smithers Chamber of Commerce, 2009.

4. "Fort Nelson Rental Vacancy Survey," Fort Nelson Northern Rockies Regional Municipality, January 2015.

5. Stephen Hume, "B.C's North: The mystique and the reality," *Vancouver Sun*, September 26, 2013.

Chapter 6

1. Staff reporter, "Employee recruitment and retention key election issues for Chamber of Commerce," Prince George Free Press, October 17, 2014.

2. BC LMI Bulletin, January 2015. Regional Analysis. www.esdc.gc.ca/eng/jobs/lmi/publications/bulletins/bc/jan2015.shtml.

3. Fort Nelson's gas is "dry," not containing other liquids. Gas found between Fort St. John and Dawson Creek has these liquids, which companies can sell separately and help compensate for lower gas prices.

4. Emma Crawford Hampel, "It's Not Just about Money: Why B.C. Employees Are Driven to Switch Jobs," *Business In Vancouver*, April 8, 2015.

5. I am aware that business owners have various opinions on having a certified workplace, but felt I would be remiss if I failed to mention the union option.

6. Resource Training Organization. Natural Gas Environmental Scan, March 2013.

7. "On the Move and Economic Update Newsletter," Initiatives Prince George, March 2015.

8. Joe Friesen, "Ottawa's new Express Entry immigration system slow off the mark," *The Globe and Mail*, April 6, 2015.

9. Speaking notes for The Honourable Jason Kenney, P.C., M.P. Minister of Citizenship, Immigration and Multiculturalism on "Moving Towards a Targeted, Fast and Efficient Immigration System focusing on Jobs, Growth and Prosperity" to the Surrey Board of Trade Surrey, British Columbia June 26, 2012.

10. "Presentation to employers," CIC, Fall 2014. http://www.cic.gc.ca/english/resources/publications/employers/express-entry-presentation-fall2014.asp.

11. "BCBC Publication: Temporary Foreign Workers in Canada: Separating Fact from Fiction," Business Council of British Columbia, July 2013.

12. "Temporary Foreign Worker Program changes explained," Canadian Federation of Independent Business, http://www.cfib-fcei.ca/english/article/6213-temporary-foreign-worker-program-small-business-advice-from-cfib.html.

13. Farahnaz Bandali, "Work Interrupted How federal foreign worker rule changes hurt the West," (Canada West Foundation, March 2015).

14. Justine Hunter, "B.C. freezes worker-immigration program as backlog grows," *The Globe and Mail,* Mar. 31 2015.

15. Gordon Hoekstra, "Northern B.C. Companies Want a Piece of Billions of Dollars in Energy Projects," *Vancouver Sun*, July 3, 2014.

16. ClickZ News staff, "Why Mobile Web still matters in 2015," *ClickZ*, January 7, 2015, www.clickz.com/clickz/column/2388915/why-mobile-web-still-matters-in-2015.

Chapter 7

1. Previously, RTA provided extra power to the provincial grid. Once the modernization is complete in 2015, RTA will need all of its formerly surplus power.

2. Sean Patrick Markey, Greg Halseth and Don Manson, *Investing in Place: Economic Renewal in Northern British Columbia*, (Vancouver ; Toronto: UBC Press, 2012).

Bibliography

Asia Pacific Foundation of Canada. *Towards a First Nations-Japan Strategy*, 2014.

BC Agriculture in the Classroom Foundation. "The Regions." *A Guide to BC's Agriculture Resources*. Abbotsford, BC: BC Agriculture in the Classroom Foundation, 2014.

BC First Nations Energy & Mining Council. *First Nation and China: Transforming Relationships*, 2011.

BC Hydro. *Site C Business Information Sessions Summary Report*, 2012.

Bandali, Farahnaz. *Work Interrupted: How Federal Foreign Worker Rule Changes Hurt the West*. Canada West Foundation, March 2015.

British Columbia. Ministry of Aboriginal Relations and Reconciliation. *Building Relationships with First Nations Respecting Rights and Doing Good Business*, 2013.

British Columbia. Ministry of Agriculture. *2011 Census of Agriculture: British Columbia Highlights*, 2011.

British Columbia. Ministry of Agriculture. *2014 a Record Year for B.C. Agrifood Exports*, April 8, 2015. http://www2.news.gov.bc.ca/news_releases_2013-2017/2015AGRI0013-000465.htm.

Brody, Hugh. *Maps and Dreams: Indians and the British Columbia Frontier*. Vancouver: Douglas & McIntyre, 1988.

Burleton, Derek. *Engaging With Aboriginal Communities Offers the Potential of Big Financial Rewards*. TD Bank Financial Group, 2013.

Burleton, Derek, and Sonya Gulati, *Estimating the Size of the Aboriginal Market in Canada*. Special Report TD Economics, June 17, 2011.

Burleton, Derek, and Sonya Gulati, *Debunking Myths Surrounding Canada's Aboriginal Population*. Special Report TD Economics, June 18, 2012.

Canada. Aboriginal Affairs and Northern Development Canada. *Aboriginal Demographics from 2011 National Housing Survey*, 2013.

Canada. Employment and Social Development Canada. *Survival to Success: Transforming Immigrant Outcomes - Report from the Panel on Employment Challenges of New Canadians*, 2015.

Canada. Indian and Northern Affairs Canada. *Aboriginal Awareness Workshop: Guide to Understanding Aboriginal Cultures in Canada.* Ottawa: 1999.

Canadian Community for Aboriginal Business. *Community and Commerce A Survey of Aboriginal Economic Development Corporations,* 2011.

Community Futures British Columbia. *Community Futures British Columbia Aboriginal Engagement Toolkit,* March 2008.

Conference Board of Canada .*Understanding the Value, Challenges, and Opportunities of Engaging Métis, Inuit, and First Nations Workers,* July 2012.

Dickason, Olive Patricia. *A Concise History of Canada's First Nations.* 2nd ed. Don Mills, Ont; New York: Oxford University Press, 2010.

Dickason, Olive Patricia. *Canada's First Nations: A History of Founding Peoples from Earliest Times.* Toronto: McClelland & Stewart, 1992.

Duff, Wilson, and Royal British Columbia Museum. *The Indian History of British Columbia.* New ed. Victoria: Royal British Columbia Museum, 1997.

Eyford, Douglas R. *A New Direction - Advancing Aboriginal and Treaty Rights,* 2015.

Eyford, Douglas R, Canada, and Natural Resources Canada. *Forging Partnerships, Building Relationships - Aboriginal Canadians and Energy Development: Report to the Prime Minister,* 2013.

Finlayson, Jock, and Ken Peacock. "Forest Sector Remains a Vital Economic Engine for BC." *Business Council of British Columbia, Policy Perspectives,* 22, no. 1 (February 2015).

Fisher, Robin. *Contact and Conflict: Indian-European Relations in British Columbia, 1774-1890.* 2nd ed. Vancouver: UBC Press, 1992.

Gallagher, Bill. *Resource Rulers: Fortune and Folly on Canada's Road to Resources.* Waterloo, Ont.: Bill Gallagher, 2012.

Gallagher, Bryan, and Thomas B. Lawrence. "Entrepreneurship and Indigenous Identity: A Study of Identity Work by Indigenous Entrepreneurs in British Columbia." *International Journal of Entrepreneurship and Small Business* 17, no. 4 (2012): 395.

Gough, Barry M. *Fortune's a River: The Collision of Empires in Northwest America.* Madeira Park, BC: Harbour Pub, 2007.

Grumet, Robert Steven. "Changes in Coast Tsimshian Redistributive Activities in the Fort Simpson Region of British Columbia, 1788-1862." *Ethnohistory* 22, no. 4 (Autumn 1975): 295–318.

Helin, Calvin. *Dances with Dependency: Indigenous Success through Self-Reliance*. 1st ed. Vancouver: Orca Spirit, 2006.

Hoffman, Kaitlin S. "Value Tradition." Master's thesis, Simon Fraser University, 2014.

Hume, Stephen. "B.C's North: The Mystique and the Reality." *Vancouver Sun*, September 6, 2013.

Johnston, Hugh J. M. *The Pacific Province: A History of British Columbia*. 1st Edition. Vancouver: Douglas & McIntyre Ltd., 1996.

Markey, Sean Patrick, Greg Halseth, and Don Manson. *Investing in Place: Economic Renewal in Northern British Columbia*. Vancouver; Toronto: UBC Press, 2012.

Meilleur, Helen. *A Pour of Rain: Stories from a West Coast Fort*. Vancouver, B.C: Raincoast Books, 2001.

Meyers Norris Penny LLP. *Best Practices for Consultation and Accommodation*, September 2009.

Morin, Jesse. "The Political Economy of Stone Celt Exchange in Pre-Contact British Columbia: The Salish nephrite/jade industry." Doctoral Dissertation, University of British Columbia, 2012.

Munro, Daniel and James Stuckey. *Skills for Success Developing Skills for a Prosperous B.C.* The Conference Board of Canada, February 2015.

Resources North. *Bridging The Divide: A Multi-Sector Approach to Natural Resources Labour Needs in Northern BC*, 2012.

Swainger, Jon. "Breaking the Peace: Fictions of the Law-Abiding Peace River Country, 1930-50." *BC Studies* 119 (1998):5-25.

Syer, Tom, and Jock Finlayson. "Understanding Economic Development and Reconciliation with First Nations in BC: The Case for Accelerating Economic Engagement." *Business Council of British Columbia, Policy Perspectives*, 20, no. 1 (February 2013).

Tennant, Paul. *Aboriginal Peoples and Politics: The Indian Land Question in British Columbia, 1849-1989*. Vancouver: University of British Columbia Press, 1990.

The Canadian Chamber of Commerce. *Opportunity Found: Improving the Participation of Aboriginal Peoples in Canada's Workforce*, December 2013.

Tsilhqot'in First Nation. *Affirmation of the Nemiah Declaration*, March 19, 2015.

Turner, Annie, and Statistics Canada. *Aboriginal Peoples in Canada: First Nations People, Métis and Inuit : National Household Survey, 2011.* [Ottawa]: Statistics Canada = Statistique Canada, 2013.

Visiting Scholar Conference. *Between Bands and States.* Edited by Susan A. Gregg. Occasional Paper / Center for Archaeological Investigations, no. 9. Carbondale: Center for Archaeological Investigations, Southern Illinois University at Carbondale, 1991.

Woolford, Andrew. *Between Justice and Certainty: Treaty Making in British Columbia.* Vancouver: UBC Press, 2005.

About the Author

Ramona Materi, MPA, MEd is the President of Ingenia Consulting. Ingenia consults on labour market and economic development issues. The firm has worked with First Nations, the natural gas, mining, solid wood, and environmental sectors, and developed workforce plans for Northwest and Northeast BC. Ramona blends 20 years of experience in consulting and facilitation with an instinctive ability to spot business trends and opportunities. She is passionate about Northern British Columbia, its opportunities, and its entrepreneurial spirit.

"Ingenia's approach demonstrated a high degree of integrity, responsiveness, and innovation. The consulting team is knowledgeable, personable, and highly professional. And the end product—the Regional Workforce Plan—is stellar."

Laurie Rancourt, President and CEO, Northern Lights College

"Ramona focuses attention on key issues and motivates decisions. Her speaking abilities are of particular mention. She presents a dynamic image and captures attention in her delivery."

Paul A. Michaud, CA, Partner - Morgan & Company

"My experiences with Ingenia have been overwhelmingly positive. They were thorough and on-time with deliverables, clearly communicated, and went over and above on the work. They provided an exceptional product and conducted themselves in a professional manner when seeking stakeholder input."

Manager, Ministry of Jobs, Tourism and Skills Training

"Ramona is a master at drawing people out, and then not letting them wander. Decisions are made: things move forward."

Bruce Stewart, CEO, Accendor Research

"I found the Ingenia team to be professional, able to work well with union and management representatives, and employees, and responsive to our suggestions and ideas."

Linda Hodgson, CHRP, HR Superintendent, Kemess Mine

Interested in knowing more?

Contact newnorth @ ingenia-consulting.com to find out more about the author, tour dates, how to book a workshop or presentation, or to order *British Columbia's New North* directly from the author.